DEPRIVED CHILDREN

Deprived Children

THE MERSHAM EXPERIMENT
A SOCIAL AND CLINICAL STUDY

By

HILDA LEWIS, M.D., M.R.C.P.

With a Foreword by
SIR ARTHUR ELLIS
and
DR. C. P. BLACKER

Published for
THE NUFFIELD FOUNDATION

GREENWOOD PRESS, PUBLISHERS
WESTPORT, CONNECTICUT

Library of Congress Cataloging in Publication Data

Lewis, Hilda Stoessiger.
　Deprived children.

　Reprint of the 1954 ed. published for the
Nuffield Foundation by Oxford University Press,
London.
　Includes index.
　　1.　Mersham, Eng.　Children's Reception Centre.
2.　Child welfare--England--Kent.　I.　Title.
[HV751.K4L4　1978]　　　362.7'4　　　77-27491
ISBN 0-8371-9070-3

This reprint has been authorized by the Clarendon Press, Oxford

Reprinted in 1978 by Greenwood Press, Inc.,
51 Riverside Avenue
Westport, CT. 06880

Printed in the United States of America

10 9 8 7 6 5 4 3 2 1

FOREWORD

THE proposal that the Nuffield Foundation should finance a pilot experiment in the reception, investigation, and disposal of deprived children was put forward by the Council of the Caldecott Community in 1944 at the instigation of the Community's Director, Miss Leila Rendel. From her experience over many years at the Caldecott Community Miss Rendel was gravely disturbed at the haphazard way in which deprived children needing care were distributed to children's homes, foster-mothers, or approved schools without any real study of their individual needs and difficulties. The late Sir Farquhar Buzzard, who visited the Community on behalf of the Nuffield Foundation at its war-time home at Bere Regis in Dorsetshire in the summer of 1944, was impressed by the desirability of this experiment. He advised the Foundation to support the application and considered that the experiment should be sponsored by the Caldecott Community with its long experience in the care of deprived children. As will appear from the Report it was indeed fortunate that this solid background of achievement and experience was available for this first study of the problems involved in a reception centre. If the Mersham experiment here described is, in its essential principles, reproduced and imitated in other counties and health regions, due credit will we hope be given to its moving spirits, Miss Leila Rendel and Sir Farquhar Buzzard.

During the ten years which have elapsed since 1944 the Mersham experiment was supervised by a committee the membership of which is given on page x. These years cover a period of acute social transition.

Of the many sections of the community whose needs have been reviewed during this period, none has received more sympathetic consideration, whether from legislators or from public sentiment, than children. And among children no class has attracted more solicitude, nor has any been more discussed, than that of deprived children. The children's reception centre is a means of dealing with a crisis in the lives of certain deprived children.

During the busy years since 1944 the merits of reception centres have been vigorously debated. These centres were first officially advocated, but later became targets for criticism. At the beginning of the first chapter will be found a fairly long quotation from the Curtis Report (1946) which commended the principle of the children's reception centre. 'We have received', said the authors, 'almost unanimous recommendations from our witnesses in favour of what are variously described as reception homes, sorting homes, or clearing stations.' And it was on the strength of this recommendation that the Children Act (1948) imposed on every county authority the responsibility of providing at least one such centre. The Home Office has since issued a memorandum quoted on p. 128 enlarging on the relevant provisions of the Children Act.

But it will be seen from the full quotation on pp. 1–2 that the Curtis Committee recommended such homes or stations for all classes of children who were even temporarily deprived of homes. The majority of such children, however, are in no sense 'deprived'; their homes are satisfactory and the event which necessitates their removal is more commonly a transient emergency than a chronic and perhaps worsening predicament. No problem of permanent disposal then arises, and there is no need for such measures as home visits, psychological testing, and other assessments which the Mersham Centre was specially designed to provide. It will be seen from p. 27 that during the year 1950, 195 children were received at Mersham; but in the same year 897 were taken into care by the children's department of the Kent County Council. In Dr. Lewis's words, 'a large proportion of these were but temporarily away from home and they presented no serious problem of disposal'. The activities of the Mersham Centre were thus more restricted and more specialized than those which the Curtis Committee seem to have envisaged. Mersham has, in fact, assumed responsibility for the most difficult cases that the county could produce. Thus, among the 500 children included in this study there were as many as 200 in respect of whom a 'fit person' order had been made before reception, and a further 75 for whom such an order was later made on the Centre's recommendation.

At an early meeting the supervisory committee agreed that an effort should be made to assess the value of the work done at Mersham. This decision was largely responsible for the delay between the publication of a report and the moment (July 1950)

Foreword

when by transfer of the Centre to the Kent County Council the Mersham experiment was formally brought to a close. The follow-up inquiry confronted Dr. Hilda Lewis, who was psychiatrist to the Centre, with an extremely difficult task. The inquiry covered 240 children (nearly half the total of 500) and as may be seen in Chapter 5 these 240 children comprised 140 in respect of whom the follow-up was by postal inquiry, and 100 who, in addition to the postal report, were personally investigated and visited by Dr. Lewis. These personal visits, which were paid to children who were widely scattered throughout the county, involved much time, travel, and preliminary correspondence. They also called for much objectivity. In her function as psychiatrist to the Centre Dr. Lewis had applied all her energies to clinical activities—to examining, encouraging, helping, and devising solutions; but in her follow-up studies she was called upon to assess with the utmost emotional neutrality the results of the efforts earlier deployed by herself and her colleagues. Readers of Chapter 5 will, we think, agree with us that Dr. Lewis has dealt with this difficult matter with praiseworthy detachment. The main findings are shown in Table 50 (p. 93), from which it will be seen that fairly conspicuous improvements are discernible in both the 100 personally visited and the 140 postally reported children. But in the light of the more searching personal inquiry the postally reported assessments, which came from foster-mothers, superintendents of homes, and others responsible for the children after they had left Mersham, were collectively deemed to err somewhat on the side of optimism and complacency. Table 50 provides key figures for those who want the simplest available answer to the simple question: what good did the Mersham experiment do? The table shows that 75 per cent. of the 100 personally visited children were in good or fair condition two years after reception compared with 40 per cent. at reception, and that the corresponding figures for the postally reported children were 78 and 36 per cent. We doubt whether more accurate assessments and comparisons than these are now possible. But, as Dr. Lewis elsewhere remarks, a formally irreproachable conclusion could only be based on a comparison of the long-term outcome (after marriage and the foundation of a family) in a sample of adults who, as children, had passed through a reception centre like Mersham, with the outcome in

Foreword

another sample of adults *in pari materia* with the first except that they had not passed through such a centre.

We draw attention to two features of Dr. Lewis's report which we think are specially valuable; the first is a finding, the second a recommendation.

The finding to which we refer provides an answer to a commonly asked question: are certain adverse conditions experienced by children in their homes (called in this report 'background patterns') recognizably connected with certain forms of abnormal conduct (here called 'patterns of disturbed behaviour')? The matter is fully dealt with in Chapter 4. Dr. Lewis confirms a general conclusion earlier reported by the American authors Hewitt and Jenkins that 'parental rejection' (a background pattern) tends to produce in the child 'unsocialized aggressive behaviour' (a pattern of disturbed behaviour); that 'neglect and bad company' (a background pattern) tends to produce 'socialized delinquency' (a pattern of disturbed behaviour characterized by gang-delinquencies); and that 'constraint' (a background pattern commonly associated with rigidity and excessive discipline) tends to produce in the child 'neurotic behaviour'. These associations between background history and presenting symptom may in part be genetically determined, for parents may transmit to their children some of the characteristics which brought difficulties and stresses upon themselves; but patterns of nurture are more manifestly responsible.

The recommendation submitted by Dr. Lewis, which we commend, is that every child whose predicament is likely to involve changes of home should at the earliest moment be assigned as the ward of a single welfare officer who would be responsible to the children's department for helping the child through the impending vicissitudes. The matter is dealt with in Chapter 6, pp. 124 and 125.

We referred earlier to criticisms of the Curtis Committee's recommendations about reception centres. These criticisms have found effective expression in Dr. John Bowlby's *Maternal Care and Mental Health* (Geneva, 1951) produced as a World Health Organisation monograph. The matter is discussed in Chapter 6 of Dr. Lewis's report. We concur with Dr. Bowlby that only as a last resort should an infant or young child be removed from

Foreword

his mother. But we think that there exists in every county a small number of parents in respect of which 'fit person' orders are imperatively necessary. The children of such parents will have suffered much before the 'order' was made. We know of no better way than that provided by the activities of a reception centre such as Mersham of minimizing the tribulations to which these children must later be exposed.

Among the events which have occurred since the Mersham experiment was begun has been the appointment of children's officers. These officers are in a uniquely favourable position both to assist the work of reception centres and to assess their usefulness. We attach importance to the views, quoted in Appendix 1, of the children's officer for Kent, Miss D. E. Harvie, on the value of the Mersham Centre. Furthermore we think that its usefulness will be manifest to anyone who reads the case-summaries of twenty-four Mersham children presented in Appendix 2.

A. W. M. ELLIS
C. P. BLACKER

May 1953

CHILDREN'S RECEPTION CENTRE
ADVISORY COMMITTEE

DR. C. P. BLACKER, G.M., M.C., D.M., F.R.C.P. (*Chairman*)

MISS ETHEL DAVIES, *Hon. Director, Caldecott Community*

PROFESSOR SIR ARTHUR ELLIS, O.B.E., M.D., F.R.C.P.

MRS. P. HAMLYN

PROFESSOR AUBREY LEWIS, M.D., F.R.C.P.

PROFESSOR A. A. MONCRIEFF, C.B.E., M.D., F.R.C.P.

MISS LEILA M. RENDEL, O.B.E., *Hon. Director, Caldecott Community*

DR. JANET VAUGHAN, O.B.E., D.M., F.R.C.P.

PREFACE

FIVE hundred children living in Kent were taken into the Mersham Reception Centre between October 1947 and July 1950. The background of these children, the homes and families they came from, their behaviour, their personalities, the measures taken to help them, and the outcome during the next two years are the subject-matter of this book.

The children came to the Centre because they were believed to need care away from their own homes: some had never had a home, or had been deprived of it when they were very young. Of these, many were referred to the Reception Centre because they could not stay where they were, their needs had to be reviewed, and some other or better provision made for them.

The Mersham Centre was the first of its kind. The aim before it was twofold—to do the best for the children, and to accumulate data which would throw light on the relation of cause and effect in their lives, deflected as they were from the normal paths of conduct and upbringing. Hence might come surer guidance on how to lessen the troubles that beset children deprived of a settled and happy home.

From the beginning there was a steady flow of children into the Centre. The predominant reasons for admission changed a little as time went on, but in the main the population of the Centre and the problems remained much the same. Administrative arrangements were tidier after a children's officer had been appointed for the county and other changes had ensued upon the passing of the Children Act in 1948, which removed financial and official complexities.

In Chapter 1 the brief history of the Centre and its procedure are set out, with an extract from the *Report of the Care of Children Committee* (the 'Curtis Report') which states clearly what a reception centre is for. In Chapter 2 the children's social situation, their parents, and their previous lives are described. In Chapter 3 their condition and conduct, in Chapter 4 the evident causes of this condition and conduct, and in Chapter 5 the outcome of what was done for them after they left the Centre are reported. A summary of the main findings is appended to each chapter. The final chapter contains some reflections that arise from a more personal and clinical review of experience at the Centre.

Preface

The Kent children studied here mostly belong to a generation whose early years were disrupted by war: they were evacuated from their usual homes in this much-suffering county; their fathers were away in the Services for years; often their mothers had worked in factories and shops, buses and canteens when the children needed their care; and, after the war, shortage of houses exposed many of them to bad living conditions. It may therefore fairly be asked how far they are a sample from which general conclusions can be drawn that would be fully applicable to children living in other counties, other countries, or other and quieter times. No social and psychological conclusions can be expressed without reference to the circumstances of place and time: but the tribulations and turns of fate in the lives of these children made it possible to examine rather more readily than in ordinary and happier families the validity of some widely held beliefs about the influence of certain stresses and privations during childhood upon the healthy growth of personality. It was also possible to see the broad effects upon the children's well-being of such measures as placing them in a foster-home. It seems likely that many of the findings set out in the following pages may have more than a local and temporary relevance.

I am indebted to many people: without their generous co-operation and keen interest the following report could not have been written. Miss Leila Rendel, who brought the Reception Centre to life and directed it with an unrivalled experience of deprived children and their needs, was an unfailing source of stimulation; with her co-director, Miss Ethel Davies, she sustained the Centre through many difficult periods. The warden, Miss F. Fretter, B.Sc., and her principal assistants Miss K. Walker and Miss Audrey Watson, served the Centre devotedly throughout its existence, and I have drawn freely on Miss Fretter's detailed and penetrating reports on the children's day-to-day conduct at the Centre. Dr. Lucy Fildes and Dr. H. J. Schleicher put their psychological findings at my disposal. For collecting indispensable material about the children's background and previous lives I am indebted to the psychiatric social workers, Mr. C. A. Wollen and Miss D. Woods. Miss Woods was further responsible for the social side of the special follow-up inquiry on a hundred children, which entailed much travelling and effort. The secretaries of the Reception Centre,

Mrs. B. Thatcher and Miss M. Richardson, handled the records and the inquiries by correspondence with exemplary attention to detail. To all the staff at the Centre I am grateful for many personal kindnesses. For general secretarial help, including much tedious coding, enumerating, and tabulation, I am much in the debt of Miss Audrey Anderson, Miss M. Kline, and Mrs. I. Kline.

Various sections of the Kent County Council, especially the children's department and the education department, were outstandingly helpful. The children's officer, Miss D. E. Harvie, gave every assistance; her steady and unmeasured support, both material and moral, enabled many things to be done which would otherwise have been impossible, especially in the follow-up inquiry. Her chief assistant, Mrs. K. E. Jamieson, and the county welfare officers helped in many ways to further the investigation. Wardens and teachers at a number of homes and residential schools both in Kent and outside gave generously of their time in providing information, and were most hospitable when Miss Woods and I visited them during the follow-up inquiry.

I must express my gratitude to the Advisory Committee and particularly to its chairman, Dr. C. P. Blacker, who has not only furthered the project in every way but given unstinted help in the revision of the manuscript. His critical comments and wise advice have been invaluable to me. To Mr. Allen Sanderson of the Nuffield Foundation I am also grateful for much assistance in preparing the manuscript for publication, and to Mrs. Hilde Fitzgerald for compiling the index. My sister, Brenda Clapham, Ph.D., has given me indispensable help in the statistical treatment of the data. From my husband, Aubrey Lewis, I have had encouragement and guidance at every stage of the work.

H. L.

CONTENTS

1. *The Reception Centre and Its Work* — 1
   1. Recommendations of the Curtis Committee — 1
   2. Locality, Buildings, and Staff — 2
   3. Welfare Authorities — 3
   4. Reception of Children — 3
   5. Conferences — 5
   6. Recommendations (*Table* 1) — 6
   7. Placements (*Tables* 2 *and* 3) — 8
   8. Practical Difficulties — 11

2. *The Children: Mode of Admission, Family Background, and Previous Personal Experiences* — 15
   1. Channels of Admission — 15
   2. Immediate Causes of Admission (*Table* 4) — 16
   3. Sex and Age — 17
   4. Family Background — 18
      (a) Social Class (*Table* 5) — 18
      (b) Family Size (*Table* 6) — 19
      (c) Family Income (*Tables* 7 *and* 8) — 20
      (d) Living Conditions — 22
   5. Parents — 22
      (a) Relationship to Each Other — 23
      (b) Social Defects — 24
      (c) Medical Histories (*Tables* 9 *and* 10) — 24
   6. Children's Personal Background — 28
      (a) Legitimacy — 28
      (b) Adoption — 28
      (c) Position in Family — 29
      (d) Previous Separation from Parents — 29
      (e) Previous Health and Education — 30

3. *The Children: Personality and Patterns of Behaviour* — 32
   1. Initial Diagnosis (*Table* 11) — 32
   2. Intelligence (*Tables* 12, 13, *and* 14) — 34
   3. Physical Condition (*Table* 15) — 35
   4. Certain Symptoms and Traits — 36
      (a) Anxiety — 36
      (b) Disturbances of Excretion — 37
      (c) Other Neurotic Symptoms — 37
      (d) Pilfering and Wandering — 38
   5. Certain Social Attitudes — 38
      (a) Excessive Demands for Attention — 39
      (b) Affective Coldness and Detachment — 40

6. Classification of Behaviour (*Tables* 16 *and* 17) 42
    (*a*) Unsocialized Aggressive Pattern of Behaviour 45
    (*b*) Socialized Delinquent Pattern of Behaviour 46
    (*c*) Over-inhibited, Neurotic Pattern of Behaviour 47
    (*d*) Slight Manifestations of the Three Main Patterns 47
    (*e*) Normal Pattern of Behaviour 48
    (*f*) Mixed Patterns 48

4. *Influence of Family and Environment on Children's Behaviour* 51
  1. Introductory 51
    (*a*) Grouping of Certain Features of Family and Environment into Three Background Patterns 52
    (*b*) Normal Behaviour 53
  2. Certain Background Features related to the Child's Recent Behaviour (*Tables* 18–29) 53
  3. Certain Background Features related to Certain Patterns of Disturbed Behaviour (*Tables* 30–35) 61
  4. 'Background Patterns' related to Patterns of Disturbed Behaviour (*Tables* 36–38) 63
    (*a*) Definition of the Background Patterns 63
    (*b*) Background of 'Parental Rejection' related to 'Unsocialized Aggressive Behaviour' in the Child 65
    (*c*) Background of 'Neglect and Bad Company' related to 'Socialized Delinquency' in the Child 66
    (*d*) Background of 'Constraint' related to 'Neurotic Behaviour' in the Child 67
    (*e*) Mixed Patterns and 'Sibling Rivalry' 69
  5. Effects of Separation from Mother 70
    (*a*) Evidence connecting Separation with Disturbed Behaviour (*Tables* 39–42) 70
    (*b*) Affective Coldness and Delinquency 77
  6. Effects of Upbringing in a 'Problem Family' 77
    (*a*) The Family Characteristics (*Tables* 43 *and* 44) 78
    (*b*) The Children: Characteristics and Behaviour (*Tables* 45 *and* 46) 79
    (*c*) Parental Attitudes and Behaviour (*Tables* 47 *and* 48) 81

5. *Subsequent Histories: Outcome* 85
  1. Introductory 85
    (*a*) Questions raised 85
    (*b*) Personal Visits compared with Postal Inquiries 85
  2. Personal Visits 86
    (*a*) Selection of Sample 86
    (*b*) Procedure: Social Investigation 86
    (*c*) Procedure: Examination by Psychiatrist 88
  3. Assessment of Follow-up Data 89
    (*a*) Method employed 89
    (*b*) Reliability of Postal Inquiries (*Table* 49) 90

Contents xvii

4. Outcome of Recommendations and Consequent Action 93
   (a) General Considerations (*Tables* 50–52) 93
   (b) Outcome related to Placement (*Tables* 53–56) 96
   (c) Outcome related to Other Recommended Measures (*Tables* 57 *and* 58) 100
5. Outcome related to Other Circumstances at Time of Reception 102
   (a) Outcome related to Attitude of Parents (*Tables* 59–62) 102
   (b) Outcome related to Previous Separation from Parents (*Tables* 63 *and* 64) 104
   (c) Outcome related to Child's Attitude to Parents (*Tables* 65 *and* 66) 112
   (d) Outcome related to Child's Age (*Table* 67) 113
   (e) Outcome related to Intelligence (*Table* 68) 114
   (f) Outcome related to Progress at School 115
   (g) Outcome related to Patterns of Behaviour (*Table* 69) 115
   (h) Outcome related to Pilfering (*Table* 70) 118
6. Outcome in 'Problem Families' (*Table* 71) 120

6. *General Reflections* 123
   1. Parents 125
   2. The Need for Reception Centres 128

APPENDIX 1. *Replies by Children's Officer for Kent to a Questionnaire* 136

APPENDIX 2. *Case-summaries: Twenty-four Children* 138

Index 157

I

The Reception Centre and Its Work

1. RECOMMENDATIONS OF THE CURTIS COMMITTEE

THE best prelude to an account of the Centre is the following extract from the conclusions and recommendations of the Curtis Committee,[1] an authoritative body which inquired into every aspect of the care of children deprived of a normal home life:

We do not consider that children who come into the charge of the authority above the nursery age should be immediately placed in the Home in which they are to remain. . . . We recommend that in the area of each responsible authority there shall be at least one reception Home. Some authorities already make this provision. Such establishments can, we are satisfied, serve several purposes. The first is medical, to see that the child is free of infection, clean, and trained in bodily control. The second is observational, to see whether the child is normal and well adjusted to society, or requires some special treatment to restore him to normality. It is essential therefore that medical and psychological advice should be available at such centres though we recognize that specially difficult cases will require closer and more specialist study than can be provided there. . . . The child should not, however, be kept in a temporary home for a moment longer than is necessary. We do not think observation should last for more than a few weeks at the outside. . . . The Homes can serve, and in our view should serve, as 'places of safety' for children needing care or protection under the Children and Young Persons Act, 1933, as well as for the first refuge of destitute children. We think also that with due precautions against the spread of childish ailments and with skilled and careful control and supervision, reception Homes could serve as the 'short stay' Homes which are needed for children whose parents are for short periods unable to look after them, e.g. because the mother is having another baby. We also think that there is a great deal to be said for using reception Homes as remand homes for small children, say under the age of 12. . . . In either case we see no reason why during the period of waiting for a decision the child should not be with other children in the reception Home and be reported on by the skilled observers there.

[1] *Report of the Care of Children Committee*, H.M.S.O., 1946 (pp. 161–2).

The Reception Centre and Its Work

It is essential that accommodation in the reception centre should be sufficient to meet not only probable average needs but the needs of a peak period—in other words that there should normally be space to spare. . . .

It was on the strength of this recommendation that the Children Act imposed on every county authority the responsibility of providing at least one such reception centre. The Reception Centre at Mersham was established before the Children Act had come into force, but it was designed to fulfil the intentions of the report in this regard and to furnish experience which might be generally useful when the Act came into effect. The medical and more particularly the psychiatric aspect of the work was considered to be of importance, and here Dr. C. P. Blacker's advocacy of children's reception centres with good psychiatric facilities in his report for the Ministry of Health carried much weight.[1]

2. LOCALITY, BUILDINGS, AND STAFF

The Centre was set up, with a generous grant from the Nuffield Foundation and the co-operation of the Kent county authorities, in October 1947. A pleasant Queen Anne house, with ample space, was taken, and as this was only half a mile from the Caldecott Community, the Directors of the Community, Miss Leila Rendel, O.B.E., and Miss E. Davies, were able to give constant supervision and help to the Reception Centre, of which also they were the Honorary Directors.

There was room for twenty-five children. The resident whole-time staff consisted of a warden, an assistant warden, a matron and an assistant matron, two teachers, and domestic staff. Often, however, there were not two teachers since it was naturally difficult to fill posts which were not recognized as entitling the holder to receive normal increments and superannuation rights: this recognition has since been accorded. The warden was, however, herself an experienced teacher with much relevant experience, so that she could fill the gap, with the help of the assistant warden, a teacher of physical training.

The psychiatrist and the psychologists worked on a part-

[1] C. P. Blacker, M.D., F.R.C.P., *Neurosis and the Mental Health Services*, Oxford University Press, 1946.

time basis, but the psychiatric social worker held a whole-time appointment.

3. WELFARE AUTHORITIES

Contact with the children's officer (appointed in 1948) and staff of the children's department of the Kent County Council was close and constant. Co-operation with them and with the officials of other departments of the local authority, as well as with child-guidance clinics, school-teachers, probation officers, and officials of voluntary bodies, especially the National Society for the Prevention of Cruelty to Children, was essential to the effective work of the Centre.

From the end of 1948 the children's officer allocated places at the Centre both for children in her own department and for those for whom the education authority was responsible. She had first claim on every bed. She sent to the Centre approximately a third of all children over 5 years who came under her care. The large number of children not sent to the Centre includes most of those who were only temporarily under care, through the illness of a parent or housing difficulties; children under 5 years, who comprised about 57 per cent. of all those coming under the care of the children's officer, were in any case seldom admitted to the Centre but went to a nursery.

4. RECEPTION OF CHILDREN

The children arrived at the Centre in the company of their parents or in charge of a welfare officer; a police escort came with those sent by a court. They were made welcome by the warden, who comforted them—many of the children were frightened and disconsolate—and explained that they would be staying only for three or four weeks; according to their age and state, they were reassured and given explanations; their questions were answered honestly, and they were told that their interests and well-being (instead of legal or punitive measures, as they often imagined) were the concern of those who would be looking after them. The parents, if they accompanied the child, were interviewed by the psychiatric social worker, who inquired into the child's history and background and did her best to establish a friendly relation with the parents. At the outset parents were often indignant and suspicious, especially when they had been prosecuted for neglecting their children though they believed they had done their best.

The full dossier of every child was sent by the department responsible for referring him to the Centre. Supplementary data of a documentary kind were collected by the social worker and incorporated into a detailed case-history which drew on many sources. These included direct oral information obtained by the social worker from teachers, relatives, various officials (school inquiry officers, inspectors of the N.S.P.C.C., probation officers) and, if the child had previously been in a foster-home, the foster-mother. The psychiatric social worker usually visited the child's home to get first-hand information: such information was especially valuable when a decision had later to be taken on whether a child, who loved his parents though they had grossly neglected him, should be allowed to go back to them.

In the Reception Centre the children were systematically observed by the warden and her assistant and by the teachers and the matron. A daily record was kept under the heads: sleep; eating; other routine habits; play and school; social and emotional responses. The entries under the last two of these heads were the most copious and provided the main material for a comprehensive review of the child's condition and behaviour which was prepared by the warden towards the end of the child's stay.

The routine of the Centre was simple. The children got up at 7.30 a.m., tidied their room, and after breakfast helped the adults with the housework, if they were old enough and willing, until they went to school at 9.30. The older children, after dinner at 1 p.m. and a period of rest or reading, returned to school from 2.15 until 4.15 p.m.; they pursued occupations of their own choice before and after tea at 4.45 p.m.; and on most days they joined the children of the nearby Caldecott Community for games or gymnastics, taking part in organized activities only if they wished. The younger children played and went for walks in the morning; they had dinner at 12.15 p.m. and then rested and played, usually out of doors. Bedtime was from 6 o'clock, according to age. At meal-times the children were grouped at small tables, and a member of the staff sat at each table and shared the meal.

Psychological testing was carried out when the child seemed to have settled down in his new surroundings: this was usually after about a week, but sometimes later. The tests chiefly used were revised Stanford-Binet, Merrill-Palmer, Gesell's norms of development, Goodenough drawing, Burt's educational attainment (reading and arithmetic), Raven's progressive matrices, and Koh's blocks. The child's attitude during tests, and especially his response to difficulties, gave valuable information. One of the psychologists made further inquiry into the child's emotional attitudes by asking him to draw anything he liked, using colours if he wished and talking while he drew.

The psychiatrist examined every child to assess his personality, hear his own story, and discover any neurotic traits or symptoms of mental abnormality. She gave him the opportunity to talk freely about his difficulties at home, at school, and elsewhere, and tried to find out his attitude towards his parents and towards any arrangements likely to be recommended after he left the Centre. She sought information showing which adults he depended on for affection, and how far separation from his parents would be harmful. Conversation, drawing (with associations and comments on the material produced), and play were the means employed according to the age and responsiveness of the child. She also made a brief physical examination; if illness was found, the child was referred to a local practitioner (Dr. Jennings) who acted as honorary physician to the Centre. Certain children were referred to Dr. Duncan Leys at the Farnborough Hospital for further paediatric investigation.

5. CONFERENCES

When all necessary observations had been made and the available records of past history and social background assembled, the child's future was reviewed at a conference, at which the psychiatrist presided over the discussion. Besides the Honorary Director and the members of the professional staff of the Centre, who attended regularly, the welfare workers, probation officers, or others who had dealt with a particular family before the child's reception into the Centre usually availed themselves of the invitation to attend and join in the discussion. Occasionally a magistrate or children's officer from

6   *The Reception Centre and Its Work*

another area also attended. The children's officer for Kent (Miss D. E. Harvie) or her representative always came to these conferences.

The conference began with a brief résumé by the psychiatrist of the child's history and social background and the reasons why he was referred to the Centre. The psychiatric social worker added social details which her special inquiries and visits had provided; her most important observations were concerned with the personality and intelligence of the parents, signs in them of illness or mental instability, their attitude towards the child, and their understanding of his problems. The children's officer, or other welfare official concerned with the family, was next asked for comments, after which the warden described concisely what she and the house staff had observed. The teachers then reported on the child's educational attainments. The educational psychologist described the findings of the psychometric tests, noting incidentally how the child had tackled the problems and his attitude towards failure and difficulties. She indicated any bent that the child appeared to possess and commented on special educational difficulties. Finally, the psychiatrist reviewed her findings about the physical and mental health of the child, briefly stated the outstanding issues that called for consideration, and asked the persons present to express opinions about the further steps to be taken. After discussion she summed up and outlined the main recommendations that had emerged. These dealt with the justification for removing the child from his home, the type of placement considered desirable, his need for medical treatment, or for special educational facilities and, occasionally, vocational assistance. A recommendation might also be made about whether he should be placed with his brothers and sisters, and whether his parents should have direct access to him and be encouraged to keep in touch by visits and letters.

6. RECOMMENDATIONS

As a rule the recommendations were put in two forms: first, what disposal would be best suited to the child's needs, and secondly, what would be fairly satisfactory if the first recommendation were impracticable because of obstacles such as lack of vacancies in suitable schools. The alternative proposal was

The Reception Centre and Its Work

necessary because there was no assurance that the first or preferable suggestion could be realized.

At the conference the discussion of each case was concise and focused on the main issue; it took approximately half an hour. The review of the main facts, and the statement of what was recommended, were then prepared by the psychiatrist and dispatched in writing to the children's officer, and, in appropriate cases, to the clerk of the court. In due course—usually within a fortnight—notice came that such-and-such action was to be taken, and the child left the Centre.

Hard-and-fast rules are highly unsuited to the delicate problem of placing each child in fit surroundings. The recommendations made at the Centre, however, showed some consistency and were on the following broad lines:

(1) Friendless children in normal mental health were recommended for a foster-home, especially if they were less than 5 years old. The same held good for mildly disturbed children who had no parents or relatives (except that some of these children needed first a spell in a small children's home or hostel where they could be introduced gradually to prospective foster-parents and could get over the upset which had preceded their admission to the Reception Centre).

(2) Children admitted with their brothers and sisters could seldom be found a foster-home to which all could go; usually they were sent to a children's home or to the care of a voluntary society, a small cottage-home being the placement most often recommended. If, however, a child showed qualities which would cause dissension or create educational problems, his brothers and sisters being free from such qualities, it was occasionally advised that he should be differently placed from the rest. The relative scarcity of foster-homes was a governing consideration here as in many other problems of placement. If nearby foster-homes could be found to receive various members of a large family who could not go back to their parents, this arrangement usually provided the best compromise between breaking up the family and sending all the children to a children's home; but it was seldom possible to find suitable foster-homes within a small radius.

Various combinations were often recommended: thus children might be sent to a boarding-school but return to their relatives for the holidays; or, if this were impracticable, they might go to foster-homes during the holidays—a practice long followed by the Caldecott Community.

A good children's home had this advantage over a foster-home for the neglected children of incompetent but affectionate parents: it did not provoke in the parents the same resentment and alienation as when they felt that the child had been taken from them and, as it were, adopted by other parents. It was much easier to get them to visit the children's home and keep up the contact with their children, whereby they could sometimes be helped materially towards re-establishing their own home, whereas visits to foster-parents often led to ill-will all round.

(3) For neurotic children and others with troublesome behaviour who were unable or unfit to return home, 'adjustment hostels' were recommended; also certain children's homes where the staff were especially successful with such children; and schools for maladjusted children. If the disorder required it, treatment at a psychiatric hospital or clinic was recommended. If separation from parents had caused or was likely to aggravate the children's symptoms it was usually recommended that they should return home and attend a child-guidance clinic.

(4) For children seriously backward educationally who came from bad homes to which return was inadvisable, admission to residential schools for educationally subnormal pupils was recommended.

(5) For children with long-standing or gross physical disabilities a period of treatment in an open-air residential school or in a convalescent home was recommended as a preliminary measure.

7. PLACEMENTS

It will be seen (Table 1) that a twelfth of the children were recommended for return home, and a fifth were recommended for a foster-home. If these figures are compared with those for children in care who are boarded out in various counties, they seem low: in Glasgow 70 per cent. of the children in care are boarded out, in Cheshire 59 per cent., in Hampshire 33 per cent.; the lowest figure for a county or county borough in England and Wales is 18 per cent. But the comparison is mis-

TABLE I
PLACEMENT OF CHILDREN
Main recommendations by diagnostic conference

Main recommendation about placement	CONDITION OF CHILDREN						TOTAL	Percentage
	Normal	Neurotic	Slightly neurotic	Psychopathic personality	Psychotic	Delinquent		
Return to parents (or relatives)	17	7	6	2	1	9	42	8·4
Foster-home	39	31	16	1	..	17	104	20·8
Boarding-school	10	12	5	1	..	15	43	8·6
Children's home	51	48	32	5	1	52	189	37·8
Adjustment hostel	..	6	4	2	1	16	29	5·8
School for maladjusted	..	..	17	3	2	27	49	9·8
School for educationally subnormal	3	2	2	..	..	6	13	2·6
Approved school	..	..	..	1	..	11	12	2·4
Others	2	..	8	..	1	8	19	3·8
TOTAL	122	106	90	15	6	161	500	100·0

leading, since the children referred to Mersham were only a fraction of all children in the county of Kent who were taken into care; and they were the most awkward fraction, with a relatively high proportion of neurotic, maladjusted, and semi-delinquent children. To send some of these children to foster-parents would have meant to court rejection after a painful trial-period, to risk incurring the resentment of the real parents, and wrecking the foster-home arrangement.

Difficulties in finding a suitable foster-home account for the ineffectiveness of many recommendations along these lines (Table 2). On the other side of the balance, however, may be counted several placements in foster-homes when this course had not been recommended: these occurred mostly when several brothers and sisters had been admitted to the Centre and efforts were made to keep them together.

Table 2 shows that altogether 76 per cent. (381) of the children were placed as recommended in spite of the scarcity of special types of accommodation.

Recommendations about other matters than placement were regularly made. They were often more important than those

TABLE 2

PLACEMENT OF CHILDREN

*Recommended related to actual placements**

Recommended placement	ACTUAL PLACEMENT					TOTALS
	Return to parents	Foster-home	Boarding-school	Children's home	Adjustment hostel, school for maladjusted, school for educationally subnormal pupils, approved school, &c.	
Return to parents	*38*	..	..	4	..	42
Foster-home	8	*73*	2	17	4	104
Boarding-school	1	3	*31*	6	2	43
Children's home	9	9	3	*165*	3	189
Adjustment hostel	4	2	1	6	*15*+1	29
School for maladjusted	6	2	1	4	*29*+7	49
School for educationally subnormal	1	..	..	5	7	13
Approved school	..	..	..	1	*11*	12
Other	5	1	..	1	*12*	19
TOTALS	72	90	38	209	91	500
Recommendations acted on	38	73	31	165	74	381
Recommendations not acted on	34	17	7	44	17	119

* Italicized figures indicate number of recommendations actually carried out.

about placement. They concerned contact with parents and other relatives, further medical care (e.g. at a child-guidance clinic or pediatric department), special educational needs, hobbies and interests (e.g. attending evening classes, art classes, trade courses), and vocational guidance. The relation with parents was invariably fostered except when deemed harmful; in which case a 'fit person' order was recommended. In addition to the 200 children on whom such an order had

The Reception Centre and Its Work

been made before they reached the Centre and the 215 children for whom no such order was deemed desirable by the Centre, there were 85 for whom it was recommended by the Centre, the court concurring in all but 10 cases. The educational requirements of children being discharged from the Centre were often conspicuous: for some the retarded classes in ordinary schools were sufficient; for others remedial teaching by an educational psychologist was called for, such as a child-guidance clinic could provide.

Recommendations referred to the period after the child left the Centre. Often it was intended that the arrangements then made should be lasting, carrying the child through adolescence; but it was sometimes foreseen that, for several reasons, the plans would later have to be reviewed. For example, the care provided might be for an interim period while more permanent arrangements were being made; or a provisional disposal might be called for by the child's particular emotional stresses at the time (as when an illegitimate child, much attached to a neglectful mother, is allowed to return to her after the mother has been put on probation). Because of the uncertainties of such arrangements, every approach by the children's department to the psychiatrist at the Centre for advice about issues arising after a child's discharge was welcomed.

The delay in placing a child satisfactorily was often considerable: 275 children went straight from the Centre to their future homes, whereas 149 had to go to some temporary accommodation for a period up to 3 months, and 76 more had to wait for a longer time—sometimes 18 months—before a suitable vacancy could be found. This happened mostly when a place in a school for maladjusted children was sought.

The duration of children's stay in the Centre is shown in Table 3. Thirty per cent. of the children stayed in the Centre for less than 3 weeks and 47 per cent. between 3 and 6 weeks.

8. PRACTICAL DIFFICULTIES

Problems were encountered which are familiar in hospital administration. Beds could not be kept full to capacity because discharges, which were usually decided elsewhere, could not be effected at the Centre's convenience, and because admissions, sometimes urgent, occurred sporadically. Consequently beds would sometimes be empty for several days, while at other times there would be an inrush of new children, greatly taxing the resources of staff and accommodation. Efficiency and a smoothly working waiting-list could only have been obtained at the expense of more important desiderata.

Sometimes there would be admitted at about the same time several anxious or rebellious children who infected each other with their unrest. In so rapidly changing a population, group loyalty and trust could not be relied on to ease the staff's task of allaying the emotional upset of newcomers.

Children who had to be away from home during their mothers' confinements or short illnesses were not normally admitted (though the admission of such children was originally suggested by the Curtis Committee), because there were more urgent claims on the Centre's beds. It was thought, moreover, that the Reception Centre with its unsettled population was not a suitable place for them.

TABLE 3

DURATION OF CHILDREN'S STAY AT THE CENTRE

(by age and sex)

Length of stay	Under 5 years		5 to 7 years		9 to 11 years		12 to 15 years and over		TOTAL		
	M.	F.	M.	F.	M.	F.	M.	F.	M.	F.	Combined
Up to 3 weeks	13	9	21	10	49	25	4	18	87	62	149
Over 3 weeks to 6 weeks	12	11	40	15	63	42	15	38	130	106	236
Over 6 weeks	10	7	19	11	28	23	3	14	60	55	115
TOTAL	35	27	80	36	140	90	22	70	277	223	500

The pangs of separation from parents and familiar surroundings could be seen in the forlorn aspect and tears of some of the children after they arrived; but in only very few did these signs of distress persist throughout their stay. The majority soon joined in games and other activities. Although a small number of children (especially adolescents) were anxious about their futures, there were few signs of genuine depression. The longer a child was kept in uncertainty about what was going to happen

The Reception Centre and Its Work

to him, the more anxious he became. There were a few isolated instances of children wandering away from the Centre.

The investigation of the child's history and behaviour was sometimes hampered by the parents' indignation at having had their child taken away from them, or by the child's distrusts and fears; but these difficulties were rare. The data collected by the Centre were, in some important particulars, fuller than those usually available to the psychiatrist at a child-guidance clinic: they provided detailed information about the child's behaviour, closely observed for several weeks when away from home. But they were less full in some other respects, such as ready information from the parents about recent events and their attitude to the child. The discrepancy was hardly discernible when the child came with his parents' full concurrence to the Centre; but it could be suspected when the child had been referred under a 'fit person' or 'place of safety' order, made because the parents had been criminally negligent. In similar circumstances the parents would probably be equally uncooperative towards the psychiatrist and social worker of a clinic, and towards anyone else whom they might regard as in league with authorities that had intervened in their homes and questioned their fitness to have their children under their care.

The chief and inescapable difficulty lies in the limited facilities available for the child if he is not to return to his own home. Administrative economies, an inadequate supply of suitable foster-homes, and gaps in the social, educational, and health services put limits to what can be provided to meet the child's needs. These limits were much narrower when the Centre was opened (1947) than they are now; hostels and schools for maladjusted children, a wider range of foster-homes and of small residential institutions, child-guidance clinics, and more educational facilities for the educationally subnormal have recently been developed. But there are still deficiencies which make it difficult to help particular children. Delays and uncertainties, which are bad for children, are the inevitable result.

During the two years and nine months covered by this report, the local authority's welfare officer responsible for a child's subsequent care had seldom had anything to do with him until his discharge from the Centre was imminent (unless the child had previously been in the care of the public authority). If the child had to be moved again a few months later, a different welfare officer might appear on the scene. This was clearly a defect. A child who is being moved to strange surroundings is under great emotional strain; he should be able to turn to a trusted and friendly adult whom he already knows. Administrative arrangements and cost may present difficulties, but everything possible should be done to ensure that the child remains in the care of one welfare officer. Steady contact with such an adult is a valuable prop to the child.

SUMMARY

1. The Mersham Reception Centre, its staff, procedure, and guiding principles, are described.

2. Recommendations made at the Centre were influenced by the high proportion of neurotic and maladjusted children who were referred by the education authority and the juvenile courts. A twelfth of the children received were recommended to return to their own homes, a fifth to foster-homes, and slightly more than a third to children's homes. Other types of placement were recommended less frequently.

3. Seventy-six per cent. of the children were placed in accordance with the recommendations.

4. Thirty per cent. of the children stayed in the centre for less than three weeks and 47 per cent. between three and six weeks.

5. Practical difficulties arose chiefly because facilities in the county were restricted and the administrative changes entailed by the 1948 Children Act coincided with the period of study.

2

The Children: Mode of Admission, Family Background, and Previous Personal Experiences

1. CHANNELS OF ADMISSION

THE 500 Kent children admitted between October 1947 and July 1950, who are the subjects of this study, fall into two main groups:

(1) Those for whom the children's officer had a statutory responsibility because they were deprived children, coming under Sections 1 and 2 of the Children Act. (Before the children's officer's appointment at the end of 1948, functions roughly equivalent to hers had been exercised by the public assistance, education, and health committees; and the children admitted through these channels are included in the children's officer's group.) This group comprised:

(*a*) Those children whose relatives could not provide for them (admitted under Section 1 of the Children Act).

(*b*) Those who came from foster-homes or public institutions for further advice about their treatment. These were children for whom the authority had assumed parental rights under a 'fit person' order.

(*c*) Those who had been newly committed into the care of the children's officer by the magistrate of a juvenile court on a 'fit person' order.

(2) Those dealt with by some other agency. This group, for whom the children's officer was not officially responsible (though she arranged their admission into the Centre), comprised:

(*a*) Children sent to the Centre by a juvenile court (though not committed on a 'fit person' order) because they were considered to need care and protection or had been placed on remand as juvenile delinquents beyond control.

The Children: Mode of Admission, Family

(b) Maladjusted or mentally disturbed children referred by the Kent education committee, at the request of a child-guidance clinic or the school medical officer. Most of these came with their parents' consent. No less than 109 children (i.e. more than a fifth of the whole) had been previously examined or treated at a child-guidance clinic, though not all of them came at the direct request of the clinic.

Two hundred and fifty of the children had been placed on some previous occasions in the care of a public authority, and 102 of them were still in public care when they were sent to the Centre. Ninety-eight other children had been newly committed to the care of the public authority under a 'fit person' order made by the magistrate of a juvenile court.

2. IMMEDIATE CAUSES OF ADMISSION

These are shown in Table 4. The obvious or main social trouble which brought about the child's admission, and was entered as such on the admission order, is here listed as though

TABLE 4

OFFICIAL CAUSES OF ADMISSION TO THE CENTRE
(by sex and age)

Official cause	Under 5 years		5–7 years		8–11 years		12–15 years		Over 15 years		TOTAL		Combined total
	M.	F.	M.	F.	M.	F.	M.	F.	M.	F.	M.	F.	
Pilfering	..	..	4	..	26	5	6	9	..	..	36	14	50
Truancy and wandering	..	..	2	..	3	2	..	3	..	..	5	5	10
Destructiveness	..	..	..	..	1	..	..	..	..	..	1	..	1
Sexual misdemeanour	..	..	..	..	1	..	..	1	..	1	1	2	3
Uncontrollable at home or school	1	1	15	3	33	21	3	12	..	1	52	38	90
Wetting or soiling	..	..	1	..	2	..	..	1	..	..	3	1	4
Moral danger	..	..	2	1	6	11	1	8	..	..	9	20	29
Neglected	14	13	15	13	24	14	4	14	..	..	57	54	111
Cruelly treated	3	2	1	1	2	1	..	1	..	..	6	5	11
Loss of parental care	12	5	19	9	12	17	..	4	..	..	43	35	78
Other causes	5	6	21	9	30	19	8	12	..	3	64	49	113
Total	35	27	80	36	140	90	22	65	..	5	277	223	500
Percentage of all children	7	5·4	16	7·2	28	18	4·4	13	..	1	55·4	44·6	100·0

Background, and Previous Personal Experiences

it were the only one; but there were often several causes at work in precipitating a child's entry into the Centre.

There was a relation between the cause of admission and the referring agency. Ninety-one of the 111 children admitted on account of neglect were referred by a court (usually after information had been collected and brought forward by the National Society for the Prevention of Cruelty to Children). Similarly, the courts were responsible for referring the eleven children removed from their homes because they were being cruelly treated, and for all but six of the fifty sent to the Centre because of pilfering.

In the heterogeneous group of 'other causes' there were twelve maladjusted or neurotic children referred straight from their homes by child-guidance clinics, and 101 children who were already living in a foster-home or public institution but were not doing well there; of these 101, 17 had been showing some neurotic symptoms, 58 had been delinquent, and 26 were children whose behaviour was satisfactory but who had to be moved for extraneous reasons.

3. SEX AND AGE

Ages and sex distribution of the children are shown in Tables 3 and 4. The proportion of boys to girls in the total sample and in the children grouped according to age or according to the reason for their admission was influenced by the policy of the Centre, and cannot therefore be taken as characteristic. It was decided from the outset not to admit boys over the age of 12 years or girls over the age of 15 years except in special circumstances. Since boys between the ages of 12 and 15 may present many of the social problems which warranted admission to the Centre, their inclusion in the total of children received would no doubt have resulted in considerable preponderance of boys over girls; the proportion of boys to girls (55·4 per cent. : 44·6 per cent.) is in any case well above that for the whole child population between the ages of 5 and 15 in the county of Kent (49·6 per cent. boys : 50·4 per cent. girls in the 1951 Census). The high proportion of boys was largely due to the greater frequency among boys, even before the age of 12, of delinquent and other socially disturbing conduct leading to their being charged before juvenile courts. The disproportion in numbers between

The Children: Mode of Admission, Family

Mersham boys and girls is almost entirely removed if the children referred directly from the courts as uncontrollable or delinquent (67 boys, 30 girls) are withdrawn from the totals.

4. FAMILY BACKGROUND

These 500 children belonged to 363 families. Two hundred and eighteen came accompanied by at least one brother or sister who was also admitted. These 218 children represented 81 families; the remaining 282 children were admitted singly. The information about the families given in this chapter has been obtained from various sources: from the parents themselves who were visited at their homes by the psychiatric social worker of the Centre and who were also frequently interviewed at the Centre; from other relatives of the child; from welfare officers, officers of the National Society for the Prevention of Cruelty to Children; from school-teachers; and from documents and correspondence. As a rule, when the children had long been in the care of the local authority, their parents were not interviewed.

(*a*) *Social class.* This was assessed from the father's occupation, in accordance with the Registrar General's classification. When the father was unknown or had never provided a home for the child from the day of its birth, the mother's social class was taken, but even this was unknown when the child had come under the care of a public authority many years earlier.

Comparison with the figures available in the One Per Cent. Sample Tables of the 1951 Census indicates (Table 5) that these children came from families which more often belonged to the Registrar General's class V than did the general male population of Kent. 'Social class' in this sense is an inference from occupational status, but it gives a statistical form to the strong impression gained first-hand that many of the children came from socially inadequate parents, of whom a few were criminals and many others had defects of character, intelligence, or health which unfitted them for meeting customary social obligations, including the upbringing of their children. The most striking instances are found in the 'problem families' separately considered in Chapter 4. The few children from families assigned to classes I and II appeared at the Centre because they had

Background, and Previous Personal Experiences

TABLE 5

SOCIAL CLASS OF FATHER, OR OF MOTHER WHEN FATHER WAS UNKNOWN

(compared with social-class distribution in Kent in 1951)

Social class	Parents of the children at Reception Centre	Percentage	All males aged 15 and over in Kent (Census 1951 1% sample)	Percentage
I	2	0·6	267	5·2
II	10	2·8	862	16·3
III	157	43·2	2,731	51·7
IV	25	6·9	769	14·5
V	122	33·6	651	12·3
Unknown	47	12·9	..	..
TOTAL	363	100·0	5,280	100·0

been thought to need residential care away from home, chiefly in boarding-schools.

(b) *Family size.* The fertility of the mothers of these children cannot be compared with available national figures such as those in the *Reports and Selected Papers of the Statistics Committee* of the Royal Commission on Population. Many of the mothers were unmarried or had not formed a lasting relationship with the child's father; the majority were still of child-bearing age and might bear more children, possibly by other fathers; and full information about stillbirths and deaths during infancy was not available in a reliable form. The data, therefore, are incomplete and the number of children in these families may be larger than recorded in Table 6. The high proportion of large families is all the more striking.

Although the number of live children born by 1946 to women first married in 1925 cannot properly be compared with our data, the figures[1] have been inserted in Table 6 because they give an indication of what the distribution of family size would have been in the general community if no children had subsequently died and all mothers had reached the menopause. The disparity between these proportions and those of our

[1] Glass and Grebenik: Analysis of the Family Census, *Reports and Selected Papers of the Statistics Committee*, Royal Commission on Population, p. 109, Table 11.

The Children: Mode of Admission, Family

families would of course be greater if the Mersham figures had included children who died, and it would be very much increased if the eventual fertility of the mothers in our group, few of whom had reached the age of 45, could be foretold.

TABLE 6
FAMILY SIZE OF CHILDREN ADMITTED TO THE RECEPTION CENTRE
(compared with figures of Family Census 1946)

	RECEPTION CENTRE			FAMILY CENSUS
	All admissions (500 children)		Children from 'problem families' only (66 families)	Live births for 1925 cohort of completed fertility. Percentage of marriages
Number of living children in family	Number of families	Per cent.	Number of families	
1	46	12·7	2	29·7
2	67	18·4	6	30·0
3	66	18·3	10	17·2
4	59	16·2	11	9·3
5	39	10·7	8	5·5
6 or more	78	21·5	29	8·3
Unknown	8	2·2	..	..
TOTALS	363	100·0	66	100·0

It is well known that the parents of 'problem families' are usually prolific—hence some of their troubles—and it is therefore noteworthy that these are not by any means the only contributors to the high fertility in our group of families.

In a sample consisting of 234 children admitted to Dr. Barnardo's Homes between 1937 and 1940,[1] the proportion (10 per cent.) of families with six or more children is smaller than in our group. This difference may be attributable to a different basis of selection, but the data are too scanty to justify any conclusions.

(*c*) *Family income*. The family income normally was that of the wage-earning parent, i.e. the father, but receipts from family allowances and pensions were included as well as any earnings by the mother. The figures given in Table 7 therefore represent

[1] *The Neglected Child and His Family*, Oxford University Press, 1948.

total weekly income, and they were calculated for the period immediately preceding the child's admission to the Centre. Though any estimate of the level at which poverty begins must be arbitrary, it is evident that many of the families are near the point at which it is difficult to provide the means of subsistence. Those worst off were the 'problem families'.

TABLE 7

FAMILY INCOME RELATED TO FAMILY SIZE

Total family income	NUMBER OF FAMILIES WITH							TOTAL	Per cent.
	Only child	2 children	3 children	4 children	5 children	6 or more children	Unknown		
Under £3 a week	5	7	1	3	4	9	..	29	8
£3–£5 a week	7	14	18	18	8	16	1	82	23
Over £5 a week	16	31	29	24	20	42	1	163	45
Nil or unknown (destitute)	18	15	18	14	7	11	6	89	24
TOTAL	46	67	66	59	39	78	8	363	100

The number of mothers engaged solely in looking after their homes was 177; 61 mothers had full-time work away from home; 37 had part-time work; and in 88 cases the situation was not clear or the children had long been in public care.

The stability of the family income of course depended on the regularity of the wage-earner's employment. Table 8 shows

TABLE 8

STABILITY OF PARENT'S EMPLOYMENT RELATED TO FAMILY SIZE

Stability of employment	NUMBER OF FAMILIES WITH							
	Only child	2 children	3 children	4 children	5 children	6 or more children	Unknown	TOTAL
Regular	24	43	44	35	24	44	3	217
Casual	1	10	11	13	4	18	..	57
Unemployed	3	5	3	2	5	5	..	23
Unknown	18	9	8	9	6	11	5	66
TOTAL	46	67	66	59	39	78	8	363

whether the chief wage-earner was steadily at work, or doing casual work, or doing no work at all at the time the child was admitted; the 66 families classified as 'unknown' were almost exclusively those whose children had for years been under the care of a public authority. It is noteworthy that 21 of the 23 families whose wage-earner was unemployed fell into the 'problem family' group.

(d) *Living conditions.* Data are given for only 285 families; the children of the remaining 78 families had been living in institutions or foster-homes for a considerable time, and the conditions in their former homes were hardly relevant or were unknown. The living conditions of 132 families were classified as adequate, of 56 as fairly adequate, and of 97 as inadequate. Visiting social workers reported about this last group of 97 families that 84 lived in overcrowded conditions and that the homes of 73 were filthy.

Accommodation was considered 'adequate' when it conformed to the standards of a residential or good working-class neighbourhood; 'fairly adequate' when it fitted a reasonably satisfactory working-class neighbourhood and the house was clean and well kept. 'Overcrowding' was recorded when there were more than two people to a room. Thirty per cent. of the families were living in overcrowded conditions, whereas only 1·09 per cent. of the whole population of Kent were living more than two per room in 1951.[1]

The families who lived in filthy conditions included necessarily a large contingent (66) of 'problem families', who had been defined in terms of dirt and neglect.

5. PARENTS

Much information about the parents of these children, though suggestive and in the individual case enlightening, could not be analysed systematically, since it was by no means sure that all the relevant details had been made known. Some of the parents, for example, were themselves illegitimate, and others were known to have been brought up in institutions or foster-homes, but such facts may not always have been disclosed, and figures on such subjects might be misleading. Attention has therefore been concentrated on the relationship between mother and father, their medical defects, and their social record (especially that of the mother).

[1] Census 1951, One Per Cent Sample Tables.

Background, and Previous Personal Experiences

Forty-five of the fathers and 41 of the mothers were dead. Some of the parents could not be traced: the whereabouts of 63 fathers and 20 mothers were unknown. They were mostly fathers of illegitimate children, and mothers who had deserted their children and vanished years ago. Since these parents were to all intents and purposes dead to their children, it may be said that about 30 per cent. of the families were fatherless and 17 per cent. motherless. In 27 families (7·4 per cent.) both mother and father were dead or their whereabouts unknown. In the 66 'problem families' none of the mothers and only 7 of the fathers belonged to the 'unknown' group, and only 8 fathers and 3 mothers had died. The higher proportion of fatherless and motherless families among the remaining 297 is explained by the fact that many children were admitted to the Reception Centre precisely because their parents had died or deserted them.

(a) *Relationship to each other.* Sixty-six of the mothers were single; 9 were widows who had not remarried, and 280 were married. Of these 280 married mothers 10 were divorced, 60 were separated from their husbands, and 22 had been widowed and had remarried at the time of their child's reception into the Centre. Thirty-eight of the wives living apart from their husbands were cohabiting with other men, who, in three instances, were the fathers of the children admitted to the Centre. The marital state of eight mothers was unknown.

The atmosphere in the home was created by the relationship between the parents (the two adults living together and looking after the children, usually the mother and her husband or 'cohabiting partner'). To classify on consistent or objective lines a human relationship that is often fluctuating and impalpable is hardly possible. However, the data supplied from many sources about these homes permitted a broad division into three categories. Leaving aside 73 families on whom the necessary information was not available because the children had been for a long time under the care of a public authority, the relationship between the parents was 'good' in 30 cases—they were living harmoniously together; 'fair' in 131 cases—they rubbed along in moderate harmony, punctuated by quarrels which were temporary or mild; and 'bad' in 129 cases—they quarrelled constantly and there were frequent scenes of brutality in which threats and abuses were exchanged in the presence of the children, who were often the ostensible cause of the outbursts. For the 'problem families' the corresponding figures were 6 'good', 25 'fair', 31 'bad', and 4 'unknown'.

(*b*) *Social defects*. The undesirable social characteristics of the parents (apart from their attitude to their children) fell into four main divisions: cruelty to spouse, drunkenness, crime, and sexual laxity. 'Cruelty' was assumed when one partner was known by the welfare authority to have ill-treated the other physically; 'drunkenness' when alcoholic excess was known to occur frequently; 'crime' when the parent had served a prison sentence for some offence other than neglecting his or her family; and 'sexual laxity' when the parent (in practice, the mother) had been casually promiscuous or had lived with a number of extra-marital partners.

Ninety-five of the fathers could not be assessed in these respects as too little was known about them. Thirty-nine of the remaining 268 fathers were cruel to their wives, 34 were drunkards, and 25 had a criminal record. The corresponding figures for the mothers were as follows: impossible to assess, 35; cruel, 5; drunkards, 7; with criminal records, 15; and sexually loose, 58.

Some of the parents had behaved towards their children in a way which is generally held to be harmful. They had neglected them, treated them harshly, without affection or with open dislike, or they had deserted them. Some, going to the other extreme, had indulged them unduly and had been over-solicitous and over-protective. The numbers of such parents are set out in Chapter 4. It is clear enough that some of the parents did not conform to the simplest moral requirements and fell well below the standards of conduct set by society. Others were foolish or sick; and a substantial number were unfortunate in the partners they had chosen. But there were also normal, kindly, sensible people among the parents.

(*c*) *Medical histories*. It was obviously impracticable to subject the parents to medical examination or to inquire closely into their medical histories, but much information was elicited which is suggestive and deserving of record. The accent necessarily lay on serious disease and defect. The physical disabilities recorded were those which had made it difficult or impossible for the parents to look after their children at home. Besides pulmonary tuberculosis, heart disease, and other thoracic conditions (bronchitis, asthma, and emphysema), they included lymphatic leukaemia, inoperable carcinoma, renal disease, arthritis, amputation after industrial injury, epilepsy, and other grave disabilities.

In some cases the parent's death from physical disease was the cause of the child's reception. The mental disabilities covered mental defect and dullness, psychopathic personality, and recent, recurring, or chronic neurotic or psychotic illness. 'Psychotic illness' was such as had necessitated admission to a mental hospital. 'Mental defect' had been certified as such. 'Dullness' was an estimate by experienced observers, who took educational attainment into account wherever possible. 'Psychopathic personality' was the diagnostic term applied to those parents whose behaviour over many years had shown rooted defects, especially in sexual conduct and in acceptance of social obligations; the diagnosis was applied with restraint, and weak and ineffectual parents, who might well have been classified as 'asthenic psychopaths', were not included.

Because so many of the children were illegitimate or had long been in the care of the local authority, their parents being inaccessible, nothing was known of the medical records of 35 of the mothers and 99 of the fathers. The frequency of medical disabilities among the remaining parents is shown in Table 9. As the same person sometimes had both physical and mental handicaps—mental defect and heart disease, for example—a separate entry shows how often such a combination occurred. Of the 99 fathers and 180 mothers who had a mental disability (with or without concomitant physical disease), 3 fathers and 4 mothers were both dull and psychopathic.

The families in which both the mother and father were known to have a medical handicap are shown in Table 10. There were 99 such cases (37·5 per cent. of the 264 families for which the relevant information about both parents was available) and they are classified according to the predominant disability of the parents.

The nature of the data and the manner in which they had to be collected make it unsafe to compare them closely with the incidence of the same forms of disability in the general population. It is clear, however, that mental handicaps were frequent

The Children: Mode of Admission, Family

TABLE 9
PARENTS' DISABILITIES

(a) Known mental and physical disabilities of 264 fathers and 328 mothers

Disabilities	Fathers	Mothers
Physical		
Pulmonary tuberculosis	8	14
Other pulmonary disease	3	6
Heart disease	1	7
Malignant growth	3	9
Other	13	14
Mental		
Mental defect	4	10
Dullness	31	63
Neurosis	16	40
Psychosis	6	36
Psychopathic personality	42	31

(b) Number and percentage of parents with known disabilities

	Fathers		Mothers	
Persons	Number	Per cent.	Number	Per cent.
With only *physical* disabilities	23	19	40	18
With only *mental* disabilities	94	77	170	77
With both *physical* and *mental* disabilities	5	4	10	5
TOTAL	122	100	220	100

TABLE 10
DISABILITIES IN BOTH PARENTS OF 99 FAMILIES

Disabilities of mothers		DISABILITIES OF CORRESPONDING FATHERS				
		Physical	Mental defect or dullness	Neurosis	Psychosis	Psychopathic personality
Physical disability	14	6	4	..	..	4
Mental defect or dullness	42	5	26	1	..	10
Neurosis	20	3	3	4	..	10
Psychosis	9	3	4	..	..	2
Psychopathic personality	14	2	3	2	3	4
TOTAL	99	19	40	7	3	30

among the mothers of the children admitted to Mersham, and that incapacitating physical illness played a smaller part in obliging the parents to concur in their children's removal from home. Mental incapacity in the parents had a more serious effect than physical incapacity on the well-being of the children and was more frequently responsible for cases of gross neglect. When the competence of both parents is reduced by illness and defect, it becomes much more likely that the child needs to be admitted to a reception centre. The conjunction of mental and physical incapacity in one parent, especially the mother, is also extremely unfavourable for the child.

The illness or death of his mother was seldom the direct cause for a child's admission: as a rule the father or other relatives tried to care for him. It was only when external circumstances or the parents' own disabilities made such a course impossible that they called on the children's officer for help or were discovered to be neglecting the child with the result that a 'fit person' order was issued transferring the child to the care of a public authority. The maternal illnesses which most frequently resulted in the child's admission to the Mersham Reception Centre were forms of mental disorder requiring that the mother should enter a mental hospital, and pulmonary tuberculosis; malignant growths and heart disease were other causes. In some such instances the mother had been living alone with the child, her husband having died or deserted her. An extreme example of sudden catastrophe was the case of a boy of 8 whose father had killed his mother out of jealousy and been sentenced to life imprisonment. In another family four young children suddenly lost their mother as a result of peritonitis after appendicectomy, and their father, himself neurotic, could not look after them properly.

Hardly any children came into the Mersham Centre because their mothers were being confined or had to go to hospital for a short period. Many such children had to be cared for by the children's department, but they were looked after in nurseries and short-stay residential homes. During 1950 the Centre received 195 children, but during the same period 897 (515 of whom were under the age of 5) were taken into care by the children's department of the county authority. A large proportion of these children were only temporarily away from

The Children: Mode of Admission, Family

home and their future presented none of the serious problems upon which the Reception Centre was usually asked to advise. Some mothers, who were of poor intelligence or depressed and worn down by the strain of caring for their children unaided, were responsible, through their incapacity, for their children's admission to the Centre, but in these cases the school inquiry officer or the probation officer would scarcely have regarded the mothers' health as the main cause for the children being out of control or neglected. One such woman, the widowed daughter of a clergyman, had become eccentric and suspicious to a morbid degree: her children were removed to the Mersham Centre because she had physically ill-treated them and let them get very ragged and dirty.

6. CHILDREN'S PERSONAL BACKGROUND

The children's past experiences accounted for much that was healthy and hopeful in them as well as for their misfortunes and failings. In Chapters 3 and 4 the relation will be examined; here some of the bare facts of their earlier lives are given.

(a) *Legitimacy.* Three hundred and eighty-one of the children were legitimate (76 per cent.), 116 illegitimate (23 per cent.), and the legal status of 3 children was unknown. These figures show a very much higher percentage of illegitimate births than exists in the general population[1] and the discrepancy is even greater if allowance is made for deaths ensuing during childhood.

(b) *Adoption.* Eighteen of the children had been adopted: they were all illegitimate. Only one of them had been placed by a registered adoption society, and in all but two instances the homes into which the children had been adopted were unsuitable. Two of the children had been treated cruelly by the adoptive parents. Until we know how many adopted children there are in the general population, it would be premature to infer that adoption without proper safeguards is likely to lead to social misfortune and a fresh deprivation of home life for the child, though the figures and experience of child-guidance clinics strongly suggest it.

[1] In England and Wales, according to the Registrar General, the illegitimate birth-rate was 42 per thousand total live births in 1937. It increased during the war, reaching a peak of 93 in 1945, but it fell to 66 in 1946 and then continued to fall to 54 in 1948 and 51 in 1949.

(*c*) *Position in family.* One hundred and sixty-seven of the children (33 per cent.) were first-born, 110 (22 per cent.) second-born, 87 (17 per cent.) third-born, and 131 (26 per cent.) came fourth or later in the family; the position of 5 children was unknown. Of the 167 first-born children, 113 (68 per cent.) were legitimate.

(*d*) *Previous separation from parents.* Evacuation from their homes in Kent, a much-bombed area, was responsible for the high proportion of the children who had at some time been away from home. As many as 316 of the 500 had been separated from their mothers. Only 103 children had lived continuously at home with their fathers. Another cause of separation was discord between the parents, which had temporarily or permanently broken up the home. One hundred and seventy-four children (35 per cent.) had been away from their mothers for two months or more and had then returned: 28 of these had been under the age of 2 and 68 between 2 and 5 years at the time. A further 142 children (28 per cent.) had been away from their mothers for many years or were permanently separated from them; for 54 of these children the break had occurred before the age of 2 and for 54 others at ages of 2 to 5 years. A larger number, 176 (35 per cent.), had been permanently separated from their fathers, mostly because they were illegitimate.

Many of these children had not only suffered from lack of maternal affection and care: they had also been moved time and time again from the substitute home in which they had been placed. There were often separate war-time residential nurseries for infants and for toddlers. The child passing from the infant to the toddler stage had to acquaint himself with new material surroundings and, in addition, with a new group of adults. When there were changes of staff the child might again pass from the care of one person to that of another. Some children showing many neurotic disorders had been exposed to as many as six or eight moves. The maladjustment of such a child cannot, therefore, be ascribed solely to the separation from his mother. In some instances a child had been accepted into a substitute family during the war; he had come to feel secure there and to regard it as his own family; when he returned to his parents he would feel a stranger or might even be rejected by them, with unfortunate consequences for his development.

The Children: Mode of Admission, Family

In all, 250 of the children (exactly half) had been taken from their own homes by a public authority at some time before the removal that preceded admission to the Mersham Centre. Thirty had been in six or more different foster-homes or institutions in turn; 27 in four or five; 80 in two or three; and 113 in only one substitute home. This subject is considered again in Chapters 4 and 5.

(*e*) *Previous health and education.* The children's past illnesses and schooling do not lend themselves to numerical statement; the data about their medical and educational status at the time they were received into the Centre are set out in Chapter 3.

Seven children had had serious illnesses—Pott's disease, encephalitis, pulmonary abscess, cerebrospinal meningitis, congenital heart-disease, severe chronic dermatitis, and deafness after bilateral otitis media; two had had an eye destroyed by injury; and one had been severely burnt. Emotional development had been manifestly affected when the children had had to go into hospital for considerable periods from homes where they had not felt secure in the affection of their parents. Epilepsy was not common: five children had a history of fits in infancy or on rare occasions later.

Educationally, the children had suffered from the abnormal conditions of war-time; they had passed from school to school, often in large classes and without the steady support of continuous home life. The facts given above about the many billets, nurseries, and the like where the children had lived also reflect the numerous changes of school: so many placements, so many schools. Essential instruction in the three 'R's' had therefore often been scrappy and imparted by different methods, with inevitable results on the children's educational attainment. These handicaps, however, were shared with most other children in Britain. The backwardness of the Mersham children, to which their teachers bore witness, must therefore be attributed to genetic and family conditions as well as to lack of continuous schooling in familiar surroundings.

SUMMARY

1. The 500 Kent children here studied were received into the Centre between October 1947 and July 1950. The channels and immediate causes of admission are stated.

Background, and Previous Personal Experiences

2. The children (55 per cent. of whom were boys) belonged to 363 families. The proportion of families in the lowest social class was higher than the proportion in the general population.

3. The fertility of these families was higher than that of the general population.

4. Their incomes and occupational stability were, on the whole, low.

5. Thirty per cent. of the families were living in overcrowded houses; in contrast, the maximal comparable figure for the general population of Kent was 1·09 per cent.

6. Many of the children's parents were dead, unknown, or out of reach. The relationship between the parents who were living together was harmonious in 10 per cent., tolerable in 45 per cent., and bad in 45 per cent. of the families. Cruelty, drunkenness, crime, indifference to their children, and sexual laxity were noted in some of the parents.

7. Among the parents medical disabilities were common. Ninety-nine fathers and 180 mothers exhibited some mental disability—defects of intellect or personality—or a definite mental illness.

8. Twenty-three per cent. of the children were illegitimate—roughly four times as high a proportion as in the general population.

9. Half the children had been removed from their own homes on some previous occasion by a public authority. Sixty-three per cent. had been separated from their mothers as a result of war-time evacuation or other causes; in 28 per cent. this separation had lasted several years.

10. The children had suffered from many changes of school as well as of home.

3
The Children: Personality and Patterns of Behaviour

IT is no easy matter in social and psychological inquiries to pass from the study of individual cases, vivid, intimate, and unique, to the impersonal search for general relations and common features. When the psychiatrist who has come close to the personal qualities and problems of 500 children in a Reception Centre has to turn these into groupings, numerical aggregates, and bald statements, the dilemma seems at first sharp: much will be lost if the nuances of the individual history and condition are submerged in classes and numbers, much will be hidden if the peculiarities and seemingly understandable sequence of causes and effects in each individual are accepted without a search for common factors. But the dilemma implies too drastic a contrast: the intimate details of the single case are needed not only to supply raw material for generalizations but also to indicate the questions that ought to be answered and the checks and provisos that must be attached to any general inference. In the following account of the behaviour and condition of the Mersham Centre children the emphasis is on the general rather than the particular, with in consequence an inevitable sacrifice of human interest: but behind it are the touching, often intricate stories of how individual children responded to the social forces and human failings and supports which attended their growth.

1. INITIAL DIAGNOSIS

After each child had been in the Reception Centre for at least a fortnight, so that the results of continuous observation and of specific psychological and medical examination were available, his behaviour was 'diagnosed'. The classification was medical in outlook: the chief categories, apart from 'normal', were 'neurotic', 'psychotic', 'psychopathic', and (a somewhat illogical addition) 'delinquent'. The need for the last category arose from those children who seemed normal in their personality but delinquent as a direct outcome of the conditions in their homes; some children were also included here who were in the main delinquent without being of psychopathic personality, though they showed some neurotic symptoms. It will be seen later in this chapter that this classification could not be adhered to when the collective data were assembled, but that it closely resembles the one eventually adopted. At the present stage of knowledge no useful classification of behaviour can be into mutually exclusive classes, and no classification can be final.

A difficult but necessary grading of the children's behaviour according to the degree of their total psychological well-being was also made by the writer. This assessment was formed after a review of all the known facts about the child's background and present condition; the criteria were too multifarious to specify.

TABLE II

GENERAL MENTAL WELL-BEING RELATED TO TYPE OF BEHAVIOUR

General mental well-being of child	Normal	Normal, with slight neurotic symptoms	Neurotic	Psychopathic personality (including epilepsy)	Psychotic	Delinquent	Total	Percentage
Very good	9	..	..	..	..	..	9	1·8
Rather good	52	5	..	..	..	2	59	11·8
Fair	49	53	2	..	..	27	131	26·2
Poor	12	48	54	5	2	89	210	42·0
Very poor	..	..	34	10	4	43	91	18·2
TOTAL	122	106	90	15	6	161	500	..
Percentage	24·4	21·2	18·0	3·0	1·2	32·2	..	100·0

The surprising appearance in the table of children with 'normal' behaviour among those whose state of general mental well-being was assessed as only 'fair' or 'poor' is accounted for almost wholly by the fact that freedom from delinquency and from neurotic, psychotic, or psychopathic evidences was sometimes found in children who showed much resentment and distress after removal from homes that were by accepted standards extremely unsatisfactory. The paradox is considered later, in the section on 'problem families'.

2. INTELLIGENCE

Many of the children whose appearance and conduct suggested that they were dull or borderline defectives proved by their response to tests that they were of average intelligence: emotional factors created the false impression. All but nine of the children were tested. Table 12 shows that there is a slight preponderance of dull children in the sample and that (apart from a slight concentration in the neurotic group) they are

TABLE 12

INTELLIGENCE RELATED TO TYPE OF BEHAVIOUR

I.Q. (revised Stanford-Binet or Merrill-Palmer test)	Normal	Normal with neurotic symptoms	Neurotic	Psychopathic personality	Psychotic	Delinquent	Total	Percentage
Below 70	5	2	2	2	2	3	16	3·2
70–89 .	25	25	30	3	1	41	125	25·0
90–109 .	59	44	46	8	1	75	233	46·6
110–29 .	22	27	9	1	2	33	94	18·8
130 or over	6	7	2	1	..	7	23	4·6
Not tested	5	1	1	..	1	1	9	1·8
TOTAL	122	106	90	15	7	160	500	100·0

distributed fairly equally in every group. The children make a somewhat better showing on non-verbal tests (progressive matrices and Koh's blocks) than on predominantly verbal ones, such as the Stanford-Binet (Table 13). The difference is no doubt in part explained by the poor opportunities of many to acquire a vocabulary in their illiterate homes—a circumstance which, together with emotional disturbances, may account for the striking discrepancies between intelligence-level as tested and educational attainment (Table 14). Often emotional insecurity (leading to fears of failure and inability to concentrate) was associated with a lack of ordinary cultural stimuli in the home, but the former alone must have been accountable—perhaps with inadequate teaching through many changes from school to school—for the failure of certain children to learn though they came from better-class homes and were of sufficient intelligence.

Patterns of Behaviour 35

TABLE 13

INTELLIGENCE-LEVEL MEASURED BY STANFORD-BINET TEST RELATED TO INTELLIGENCE-LEVEL MEASURED BY PERFORMANCE TESTS

(*Chronological age* = *I.Q.* 90–109)

Mental age (revised Stanford-Binet test)	MENTAL AGE ASSESSED BY PERFORMANCE TESTS			TOTAL
	Above chronological age	Equal to chronological age	Below chronological age	
Above chronological age	45	9	6	60
Equal to chronological age	45	46	28	119
Below chronological age	9	17	54	80
TOTAL	99	72	88	259

TABLE 14

STANDARDS ATTAINED IN READING AND ARITHMETIC RELATED TO TESTED INTELLIGENCE*

Intelligence quotient	READING AGE			ARITHMETIC AGE		
	Above mental age	Equal to mental age	Below mental age	Above mental age	Equal to mental age	Below mental age
Below 70	1	1	12	2	..	12
70–89	16	9	81	8	..	95
90–109	17	19	130	3	1	166
110–129	9	8	42	1	..	55
130 or over	4	1	13	..	..	18
TOTAL	47	38	278	14	1	346

* Children were not tested for educational attainment during the first six months after the Centre opened, or if they were under 5 years of age.

3. PHYSICAL CONDITION

This was determined by a rapid examination, which included measurement of height and weight, and a more detailed examination where necessary: several children were referred to the children's department of the Farnborough Hospital (Dr. Duncan Leys) and others, who needed immediate treatment of surgical or infectious conditions, were referred to the local hospital.

Apart from minor disorders, such as a cold, impetigo, or

chronic nasal discharge, very few of the children were suffering on admission from severe or definite illnesses: one had a chronic tuberculous abscess in the cervical glands, another had bronchiectasis, another had acute otitis media, and a few had whooping-cough, scarlet fever, or measles when admitted. Two were blind in one eye, another was largely incapacitated by congenital heart-disease, and another had severely impaired hearing.

A three-point rating of the children's physical condition was made: the chief criteria were the child's weight and general nutrition, freedom from chronic infections or signs of debilitating illness, and condition of skin, teeth, and mucous membranes.

TABLE 15

GENERAL MENTAL WELL-BEING RELATED TO PHYSICAL CONDITION

General mental well-being	PHYSICAL CONDITION			TOTAL	Per cent.
	Good	Fair	Poor		
Good	47	13	8	68	13·6
Fair	64	45	22	131	26·2
Poor	123	101	77	301	60·2
TOTAL	234	159	107	500	..
Percentage	46·8	31·8	21·4	..	100·0

Three-quarters of those who were in poor physical condition were also in a poor state of mental well-being. In a separate analysis of the children's weight in proportion to their height and age (according to Wood's tables), there were (omitting 73 on whom the measurements were not made) 163 who were 2 lb. or more below average weight, 124 who were within 2 lb. of average weight, and 140 who were 2 lb. or more above average. It is necessary to be cautious in drawing conclusions from such data, because of the wide range of weight in healthy children in the general population and the well-known difficulty of determining nutritional status.

4. CERTAIN SYMPTOMS AND TRAITS

(a) *Anxiety.* This almost universal characteristic of children whose lives have been disturbed in some way could be attri-

Patterns of Behaviour 37

buted, in two-fifths of the Mersham children, to the natural distress and uncertainty aroused by their having to leave home to come to the Centre; it was readily allayed by sympathetic discussion and reassurance. In the remaining 300, who are distributed among the 378 disturbed children shown in Table 11 (p. 33), the anxiety reached neurotic intensity, often aggravated by the child's recent vicissitudes—being brought before a court, for example, or being removed from home against the parents' will. The anxiety of these 300 children took forms familiar at child-guidance clinics: they were restless, uneasy, moody, and sensitive; they gave up any task that demanded attention and sustained effort; they could not face overt failure; they often slept poorly and were prone to terrifying dreams and morbid fears. One hundred and thirty-three children showed these signs of anxiety in a severe form, 116 showed them moderately, and 51 were mildly affected. Anxiety was a very frequent characteristic of children who wet the bed and of those who had a history of pilfering: 112 of the 162 children who were given to wetting the bed showed anxiety, as did 103 of the 134 pilferers; it could be maintained that enuresis and pilfering are among the many manifestations of an anxiety-state in children.

(*b*) *Disturbances of excretion.* Rather against expectation, many children who were reported to have wet the bed before admission did not do so during their stay at the Centre; no doubt the new routine and the relief from disturbing home influences brought this about. Omitting children under the age of 3 (whose enuresis might have been the result of faulty training under primitive housing conditions) there were 162 who had wet the bed often enough before coming to the Centre for it to be regarded as more than an occasional lapse. Thirty-seven of these had also at some time soiled their clothes, bedding, or furniture with faeces, though only two persisted in this while at the Centre: this encopresis had been commoner among aggressive and destructive children than others. Delinquency and enuresis were not particularly associated: the latter symptom occurred in the same proportion (a third) of children who pilfered as of children who did not.

(*c*) *Other neurotic symptoms.* Nail-biting was very common, sometimes to the point at which the finger-tips were sore and deformed. Tics and mannerisms, masturbation, and obsessional traits were reported, but were not obtrusive: thus, mild obsessional tendencies were often detectable, but only in three children could they be regarded as definite symptoms.

(*d*) *Pilfering and wandering.* These two disturbances of conduct, like others just mentioned, were less evident after admission than before. Nine children wandered away, most of them merely on one occasion; and the only children who pilfered at the Centre were some who had formed habits of stealing and lying over a long period during which they had been deprived of security, affection, and healthy outlets. One hundred and thirty-four children were known to have pilfered before admission: in 37 of these the pilfering had been trifling and infrequent, in 26 serious because of repeated acts or on account of the value of the objects taken, and in the remaining 71 thefts had either been frequent and trifling or isolated and serious. Only rarely did the children give a reason for their misdemeanours; the majority gave no motive or a transparently inadequate motive, the causes of their behaviour being too complicated and obscure for a child to recognize. As earlier remarked, anxiety was frequent: 77 per cent. of the pilferers showed anxiety (apart from anxiety about the consequences of their offence) as against 54 per cent. of the children who had not pilfered.

5. CERTAIN SOCIAL ATTITUDES

A child's relationship to people is an index of his emotional health and development. Elusive and varying, it cannot be measured or confidently labelled; but gross disturbances can be detected, and there are some forms of social maladjustment which clinical experience and psychopathological theory have singled out for closer scrutiny. Detailed discussion and speculation are here inappropriate: but it is necessary to indicate the forms in which disturbances of social attitude and feeling were manifested in these children. Something must also be recorded (Chapter 4) about the circumstances that preceded or accompanied the development of maladjustment, because it is commonly believed that a child deprived of the affection and security of a home will be handicapped in developing a healthy attitude to people.

Patterns of Behaviour 39

(*a*) *Excessive demands for attention.* To want to be noticed is so common an attribute of young children that it cannot be regarded as abnormal unless it persists and is displayed in season and out of season. Mild exhibitions of it, in children who had been indulged by overfond parents or who had come from homes that gave no scope to their intelligence, energy, and emotional needs, often faded away in more suitable conditions. For example:

> A 5-year-old girl, whose father was a criminal and whose mother was a dullard, had been brought up in an institution until she was 4 and then taken by an over-indulgent foster-mother, herself an orphanage-bred girl. The child was violent to other children, screamed when she could not get her own way, and was importunate in seeking the constant interest of her foster-parents. Admitted to Mersham, she gave at first the impression of a self-possessed and precocious child, deliberately using voice, smiles, and gesture to please and impress adults. If she could not get what she wanted from them, however, by these wiles and charms, she went into a tantrum and would not eat. On the other hand she looked after herself well and was quick to size people up: she got on less well with children than with grown-ups. When she was moved from her previous foster-home to another in which there was a more sensible attitude and real affection, her waywardness and demands for attention disappeared.

The ways in which the need was exhibited varied according to the child's age; a young child, perhaps brought up from birth in nurseries, would run indiscriminately from person to person asking to be fondled, whereas an older child would try in every situation to draw attention to himself by showing off, making faces, offering irrelevant comments, and so on. Many of these attention-seeking performances were associated with boasting, jealousy of other children, and a desire to dominate or displace them. A few of the younger children who showed this feature had, before admission, also wandered away and forced themselves on the attention of complete strangers.

These children were often severely disturbed in other ways: they wet the bed and in some cases soiled themselves; they did not join in games in the way appropriate to their age, but would resort to babyish play based on fantasy, or would boss and bully the others.

An example of this mixture of infantile and neurotic behaviour was a little girl, nearly 8 years old. She was an illegitimate child, placed at the age of 1 year with a relative who had four children of his own: he and his wife did not succeed in liking and trusting the child, though they adopted her, and her presence was resented by one of her foster-brothers, older than herself. She began to pilfer, wander from home, and talk to any strangers who would listen; finally she came before a juvenile court for having run off with babies in their prams in order to play with them in the park. Enuresis, by day as well as at night, and encopresis were also reported. When she came to Mersham, she played a great deal with dolls, treating them as much-loved infants; she clung to the members of the staff, chattering incessantly, anxious to work for them and show her affection, whereas in a group of other children she was timid, tense, and out of her element. Her incontinence of urine did not cease while she was in the Centre or at the school for maladjusted children to which she next went.

Demands for attention were rare among neglected children who came from dirty homes. Indeed in a few of these products of the 'problem family' the reverse behaviour was exhibited: they were shy, avoiding adults as much as they did other children. No doubt ostracism at school and in the home neighbourhood had promoted this withdrawal from the risks of having their feelings hurt and their advances rejected.

One little boy from a very poor home, much despised by the families near by, had repeatedly played truant from school, where his ragged clothes and dirt put him to shame and the other boys would not play with him. At Mersham he kept entirely to himself, at first regarding all adults with fear and suspicion; but after a while he became more friendly and trusting.

(*b*) *Affective coldness and detachment.* This quality of emotional indifference, which is often striking in adult criminals, has played a prominent and controversial part in psychiatric literature, especially in German writings of the last seventy years dealing with psychopathic personality and 'moral insanity'. Since Ziehen,[1] following on Emminghaus and Binswanger, drew attention to it, the affective poverty or crippling seen in some children who commit offences has been examined by German and, more recently, by American and English investigators.

[1] Th. Ziehen, *Die Geisteskrankheiten des Kindesalters*, Berlin, 1917.

Some of the latter have been mainly concerned with the psychological causes of this abnormal emotional condition, or have come across it in the course of inquiries into the harmful effects of institutional upbringing. Their descriptions mostly repeat the German accounts of what *gemütlose* or *gemütsarme Psychopathen* are like, but their emphasis on the link between this emotional defect and a preceding deprivation of normal home life and maternal affection introduces a new and important theme, of obvious relevance to the Mersham children. Thus Bowlby[1] (who has published the most recent, comprehensive, and documented review of the subject) is convinced that prolonged deprivation in the early years of life is specifically connected with the later development of an 'affectionless psychopathic character': he applies this term to children who 'appear emotionally withdrawn and isolated. They fail to develop libidinal ties with other children or with adults and consequently have no friendships worth the name. It is true that they are sometimes sociable in a superficial sense, but if this is scrutinized we find that there are no feelings, no roots in these relationships.' (In this chapter only the descriptive features of the condition will be dealt with, the causal aspect being reserved for Chapter 4.)

Nineteen of the 500 children were judged to show morbid lack of affective responsiveness. The judgement is, however, inevitably subjective, as can readily be discerned in the last sentence of the quotation from Bowlby. Typical descriptions of these children are: 'Expressionless face.... Affect seems diminished although he is not depressed. Has a curiously detached and impersonal way of talking about his foster-parents and other people'; 'unresponsive ... shows little emotion and warmth of feeling'; 'undemonstrative and shallow. Veneer of politeness but seems fundamentally indifferent.'

It would be misleading to imply that all the nineteen children showed a universal lack of affective response to adults and children: this was most exceptional. In the majority their detachment and devices for avoiding emotional involvement were selective, being displayed more towards some individuals or classes of people than others, and their mostly unemotional behaviour was punctuated by lively expressions of feeling, such as an outburst of temper. Most commonly, shallow and

[1] J. Bowlby, *Int. J. Psycho-Anal.*, 1940, **21**, 154.

superficial affect was associated with evasiveness, pilfering, lack of concentration, and efforts to attract the attention of adults. Milder forms consisted in coolness and reserve towards adults but friendly co-operation with other children, who seemed to give the child and receive from him in return the affection he could not exchange with adults. More often, however, the children of this group were on bad terms with other children, sometimes showing towards them the same calculating dislike or indifference as towards adults and sometimes bullying them. The conjunction of superficial unresponsiveness and thinly veiled hostility to adults was particularly seen in children in whom aggressive and destructive behaviour or a compunctionless cruelty was the outstanding problem.

6. CLASSIFICATION OF BEHAVIOUR

The abnormal behaviour of children cannot easily be classified: no satisfactory categories have yet been established for clinical or social purposes. It is difficult enough to distinguish abnormal from normal behaviour, because a child's past and present surroundings have first to be taken thoroughly into account. To measure the extent of any abnormality is still more difficult (except where mental deficiency is the main trouble). In most studies abnormal behaviour has been classified partly on a medical basis, using clinical divisions close to those of the psychiatry of adults, and partly on a social basis, with stress on the forms of juvenile delinquency. Inevitably these divisions overlap. Such a scheme, however, has in practice been taken for granted, as being in accordance with experience and convention. Among the few investigators who have approached the problem more systematically, L. E. Hewitt and R. L. Jenkins[1] are outstanding: their classification, with minor changes, has here been adopted as most appropriate to the needs of the inquiry. A brief account follows of what it is and how they arrived at it.

Hewitt and Jenkins examined the items of deviant behaviour listed in the case-records of 500 children seen at the Michigan Child-Guidance Institute. Statistical analysis, by means of multiple correlations, revealed three main sorts of behaviour in each of which

[1] L. E. Hewitt and R. L. Jenkins, *Fundamental Patterns of Maladjustment. The Dynamics of Their Origin*, State of Illinois, 1946.

Patterns of Behaviour

certain activities or traits occurred so frequently together that it could reasonably be assumed that they formed a consistent pattern. The three patterns were: 1. *unsocialized aggressive behaviour*; 2. *socialized delinquent behaviour*; 3. *over-inhibited behaviour*. The first of these comprehended the defiant aggression seen in children who disregard the rights of others: its outstanding features are acts of violence, cruelty, starting a fight, open defiance of authority, malicious mischief, inadequate feelings of guilt. The second pattern, 'socialized delinquent behaviour', included conduct in which the child is on good terms with other children of his own group or gang, though he offends against the codes of society at large and shows no respect for the rights of people outside his own group: the outstanding features of this behaviour are association with undesirable companions, gang activities, co-operative stealing, furtive stealing, habitual truancy, running away from home, staying out late at night. In the third pattern, 'over-inhibited behaviour', the child exhibits an incapacity for showing satisfactory emotional responses: the chief characteristics are seclusiveness, shyness, apathy, worrying, sensitiveness, submissiveness.

No child's behaviour can be expected to conform in every detail to one of these patterns; but at least three of the listed features of each pattern should be detectable. Using this criterion (the presence of three or more of the features) Hewitt and Jenkins were able to classify 40 per cent. of their 500 children; the rest did not fit into their three patterns. This might be counted a severe indictment of their classification if the patterns of behaviour were mutually exclusive or were the outcome of independent variables. This is not so. Nevertheless, the large proportion of children whose behaviour could not be fitted into one of the three patterns reduces the practical value of the classification, and has made difficulties in applying it to our sample. But it still has a more solid and objective basis than most others and has been adapted without serious modification to the needs of this inquiry. Hewitt and Jenkins, moreover, subjected their tripartite classification to a further stringent test, which confirmed its usefulness. Using statistical checks, they sought to relate their three main patterns of behaviour to circumstances in the social and family backgrounds of the children studied. Again on the whole they succeeded in this search for causal conditions. The outcome of a similar examination of our material is described in Chapter 4.

The 500 Mersham children were not necessarily referred, as children are, to child-guidance centres because their behaviour caused concern. Consequently, it was to be expected that many of them would not show any disorders of behaviour. This expectation was borne out: 119 children could be regarded as normal in behaviour. There were also 155 children whose abnormal behaviour was so transient or unobtrusive that it could not justly be classified in one of the three patterns, though a trend towards misbehaviour was evident. Thirty-seven other children, who were particularly disturbed, showed combinations of the three main patterns which prevented their being ascribed to any one. The classification into main patterns and subordinate or mixed groups is shown in Table 16.

TABLE 16

PATTERNS OF BEHAVIOUR AT RECEPTION

Pattern of behaviour	No. of children	Approx. per cent.
Normal	119	24
Unsocialized aggressive	52	10
Socialized delinquent	57	11
Over-inhibited, neurotic	80	16
Slightly 'unsocialized aggressive'	25 ⎫	5
Slightly 'socialized delinquent'	19 ⎬ 155	4
Slightly 'over-inhibited, neurotic'	111 ⎭	22
Mixed patterns	37	8
	500	100

The relatively high proportion of children (155) with only mild departures from normal behaviour is striking. Moreover, in all groups there was an admixture of features of behaviour belonging to another pattern: for example, neurotic 'over-inhibited' traits appeared in a predominantly aggressive pattern. This was most evident in younger children, whose immaturity seemed to betray itself in the open battle between an infantile desire for pleasure, aggressive feelings, and inhibitory forces preventing their free expression. As already noted (Table 3, p. 12), young children were in the majority, especially among the boys, only 8 per cent. of whom were over 11. Fifty per cent. of the 277 boys were between the ages of 8 and 11 years and 42 per cent. under the age of 8: the corresponding figures for the 223 girls were 40 per cent. and 28 per cent.

Moreover, there were more young children in the normally behaved than in the abnormally behaved group. The 381 children with abnormal behaviour (see Table 17) comprised the

TABLE 17
PATTERNS OF BEHAVIOUR AT RECEPTION
(by age)

Pattern of behaviour	Under 8 years	8–11 years	12–15 years	Over 15 years	TOTAL
Normal	61	33	25	..	119
Unsocialized aggressive	11	27	11	3	52
Socialized delinquent	4	37	15	1	57
Over-inhibited, neurotic	25	43	12	..	80
Mixed	13	21	3	..	37
Mildly delinquent	9	24	9	2	44
Mildly neurotic	55	45	11	..	111
TOTAL	178	230	86	6	500

following age-groups: under 5, 9 per cent.; 5–7 years 22 per cent.; 8–11 years 52 per cent.; 12–15 years 16 per cent. The corresponding figures for the children with normal behaviour were: under 5, 25 per cent.; 5–7 years 27 per cent.; 8–11 years 28 per cent.; 12–15 years 21 per cent. The bulk of normally behaved children were members of whole sibships who had been removed from home for 'care and protection'; hence it may be inferred that the unusual age-distribution in this group only reflects the readiness of social agencies to intervene on behalf of neglected families if the children are mostly quite young.

The normal children will be discussed in Chapter 4.

(*a*) *Unsocialized aggressive pattern of behaviour.* All but three of the fifty-two children in this group showed anxiety or insecurity; they were uneasy and could not concentrate well on tasks or play.

Besides the aggressive traits characteristic of the group, these fifty-two children showed features which could be sub-grouped as follows:

(i) Twenty of the children were excessively eager for affection from adults but were easily frustrated and discouraged, then showing hostility to adults.

A little girl of 8 was at first dejected and silent, but became more cheerful: she would, however, whine and lie on the ground moaning or screaming, demanding attention and showing much resentment if she could not get it.

Another of the same age was jealous and quarrelsome with other children; but she was ingratiating with adults unless she had been reprimanded, when she became sulky and angry.

Still another girl was at first uncontrollably defiant if given the mildest order, e.g. to come to a meal or go to bed, though later she became agreeable and compliant.

(ii) Ten of the children seemed to lack the capacity to show affection. Besides this defect, sometimes covered by a veneer of politeness, they showed cruelty to animals and destructiveness. Often it could be seen that their coldness of manner was associated with actions calculated to gain personal advantage. Eight of these ten children wet the bed.

(iii) Seventeen children were not only aggressive but solitary, sensitive, and much of the time timid. One had had an acute though mild psychosis some months before. Another had had outbursts of temper, had smashed things, and occasionally stolen; he played alone though occasionally he could be induced to join in a group game, becoming rough if no adult was present; he blinked a great deal and had a sniffing tic.

(iv) Five children were only mildly disturbed in behaviour: though aggressive, they were not persistently so; sometimes their hostility centred on a parent or stepfather.

One boy of $11\frac{1}{2}$ had lost his father when he was 5, and had come under the harsh discipline of a man with whom his mother lived. This boy, who was admitted to the Centre after he had stolen a bicycle, was discontented with himself, quick to take offence, and would try to bully adults or other children; he would noisily refuse to do his class work. But in lessons which interested him and in which he could do well he was pleasant, and he was not unpopular with the other children. During the later part of his stay he developed an easy, friendly relationship with adults and accepted responsibility in a practical sensible way.

(*b*) *Socialized delinquent pattern of behaviour.* Of the fifty-seven children whose behaviour was so classified, twenty-seven showed the typical delinquent behaviour accompanied by aggressive traits such as defiance of authority, bullying, quarrels with other children, and troublesome outbursts of violent temper and destructiveness. In these twenty-seven there was, in short, an admixture of the traits typical of the first-named pattern, 'unsocialized aggressive behaviour'. Admixture of the third pattern, 'over-inhibited, neurotic behaviour', was also common among the fifty-seven children in this group, who wandered,

Patterns of Behaviour

pilfered, and consorted with delinquent companions in gangs. Indeed, the group contained only four who showed no anxiety and only twenty-three who displayed trifling or mild neurotic symptoms. The majority showed such features as restlessness, inability to concentrate, feelings of inadequacy, a tendency to retreat when faced with difficulties, disturbed sleep, morbid fears, excessive nail-biting, thumb-sucking, and desire for attention from adults. Fourteen wet the bed, and five of these also soiled themselves with faeces. Because they evaded difficulties and took the easy way, they seemed lazy, self-indulgent, and untruthful: they often went to fantastic lengths in denying their misdemeanours, especially if they had been stealing.

Their delinquency was as a rule trifling by ordinary standards: they pilfered objects of little worth. But the persistency of their anti-social behaviour (one child, 7 years old, had been charged with larceny twenty times) was a grave feature. Two children stole considerable sums of money, e.g. a teacher's pay-packet containing a month's salary. Ten children had been concerned in mild sexual misconduct.

(*c*) *Over-inhibited, neurotic pattern of behaviour.* Within this group of 80 children two sub-groups could be discerned: 47 who were seclusive, submissive, timid, moody, and with a tendency towards obsessional behaviour; and 33 who were insecure, anxious, and prone to seek the attention of adults while showing jealousy of other children. The first sub-group of 47 contained a higher proportion of children who were sometimes aggressive, quarrelsome, and defiant (12, against 8 in the second); whereas the second sub-group of 33 included relatively more children who slept badly, or wet the bed (25, against 14 in the first sub-group). In the inhibited seclusive sub-group there were six children who seemed incapable of showing affection, or arousing it; one of these exhibited a mute autistic syndrome, and another's condition likewise aroused suspicion of early schizophrenia.

(*d*) *Slight manifestations of the three main patterns.* It is a moot question, when attempting to classify some aspect of the complex continuum of human behaviour, whether milder forms of aberrant behaviour should be regarded as normal or not, since the line of division is so indistinct and arbitrary. It has seemed more informative here to deal with them as separate groups, intermediate between the normal and the decidedly abnormal.

These 155 children showed little disturbance of personality or conduct, especially while under observation at the Mersham Centre. Their delinquent acts had been trivial, their aggressiveness superficial, their anxiety mild and easily allayed. Their behaviour had, however, caused concern and, although their circumstances often accounted for this, it would be misleading to group them with the wholly normal children.

(*e*) *Normal pattern of behaviour.* The 119 children in this group were well adjusted, and free from social and medical signs of trouble.

(*f*) *Mixed patterns.* The conduct of thirty-seven children could not be assigned clearly to any main pattern. Six showed a combination of features of the two groups 'unsocialized aggressive' and 'socialized delinquent': they were decidedly hostile and defiant, and they pilfered with other children or committed other offences in a gang. Twenty-five others were antagonistic to their companions, persistently quarrelling with other children, sometimes attacking and bullying them; two of these were particularly cruel and without remorse for their cruelty. Most of these twenty-five children were sensitive, insecure, disturbed in their sleep, sometimes timid, afraid of the dark, resentful if other children received attention (but not openly seeking it for themselves), and prone to tics and mannerisms. Many had pilfered and wandered away in the period before admission, but they seldom engaged in gang activities, and they stole mostly from their own homes or from children whom they threatened. Ten of these twenty-five children habitually wet the beds at night; two of them also soiled their clothes with faeces: in all, the 'mixed' group included fifteen enuretic children, four of whom were also encopretic. A further six children displayed a variety of disturbances of conduct including sexual offences and hysterical self-injury; three of these were physically handicapped, as by the loss of an eye.

Because many of the children in this 'mixed' group got on so badly with other children, it was at school that their conduct first attracted attention. The open conflict between them and their schoolfellows led to their being considered maladjusted.

The following are brief examples of the behaviour of children in this 'mixed' group.

An illegitimate child whose infancy had been chequered by a head-injury, the death of his twin brother at the age of 3, and the misconduct of his mother, had begun to steal when he was 4; he became destructive, wandered away from home, constantly interfered with other children, and, at the age of 8, was eventually brought before a court for stealing and wilful damage to property. When sent by the court to Mersham, he looked frightened and unhappy, and while there was willing to do things for adults but was noisy and disturbed other children. He wet the bed every night, and occasionally wet himself by day and smeared odd corners of the house with faeces.

Another boy, whose mother had always shown her disappointment that he was not a girl and had openly preferred his younger brother, began to attack this brother and then other children. Whining, restless, and solitary at first while at the Centre, he became more confident in the company of adults but towards children was aggressive and boastful; he too wet the bed and soiled himself with excreta.

Another child, a girl with congenital heart-disease, had become accustomed to wander from home, talking to strangers and begging money; admitted to the Centre at the age of 10, she was over-affectionate and lively with adults, unless they required her to do anything exacting, when she would change colour and become stubborn and resentful; with children of her own age she was on bad terms, wanting the best of everything for herself.

SUMMARY

1. A quarter of the children—24·4 per cent.—admitted to the Centre were normal in behaviour and general mental condition. Twenty-one per cent. showed slight and 18 per cent. severe neurotic symptoms. Thirty-two per cent. were delinquent in some degree, and 4 per cent. either psychotic or psychopathic.

2. Twenty-eight per cent. had an intelligence quotient (Stanford-Binet) below 90. Nearly 47 per cent. were of average intelligence and 23 per cent. had an intelligence quotient above 110. Their success in performance tests was greater than in verbal tests; their attainment in reading and arithmetic was poorer than their age or intelligence warranted.

3. Twenty-one per cent. were in poor physical condition; 38 per cent. were under weight.

4. The conspicuous symptoms before admission were anxiety, enuresis, pilfering, and wandering.

5. Social attitudes included excessive demands for attention and affective coldness. The latter characteristic was observed in nineteen children.

6. The children's general behaviour was classified according to the patterns described by L. E. Hewitt and R. L. Jenkins. Ten per cent. conformed to the pattern of 'unsocialized aggression'; 11 per cent. to the pattern of 'socialized delinquency', and 16 per cent. to the pattern of 'over-inhibited neurosis': milder forms of the three patterns, not much removed from normal behaviour, were observed in 5 per cent., 4 per cent., and 22 per cent. of the children respectively. Eight per cent. of the children exhibited mixed patterns of behaviour. The remaining 24 per cent. were children with normal behaviour.

7. The abnormal patterns of behaviour are described and illustrated.

4

Influence of Family and Environment on Children's Behaviour

1. INTRODUCTORY

IT would be foolhardy to expect that, from the study of these children's lives, simple causes could be discovered to account for their mode of behaviour. Even the most sanguine investigator could hope only to see broad connexions, suggesting rather than demonstrating that particular adverse influences may bring about characteristic deviations of conduct. So far as hereditary influences are at work—and they may be greatly so—the inquiry could not throw light on them because the data are insufficient (with especially large lacunae for the numerous illegitimate children), and it is impossible in most instances to sort out the genetic from the environmental and psychological influences supplied by the parents. Though the environmental factors are therefore dealt with exclusively in this chapter, it is by no means implied that the hereditary determinants are negligible: it would be indeed strange if so many maladjusted, dull, neurotic, and psychopathic parents as are included in this series did not hand on some of their defects to their children.

The background of these children has already been described in Chapter 1. It had been subject to the general turmoil and privations of war-time, which fell particularly heavily on children separated from their parents. The most deprived, in the now familiar usage of this word to denote children who have not had the continuous affection of their parents and the security of a settled home, were those who had been in public care, in some cases since infancy. What the attitude of their parents had been could often only be conjectured, but, when the child had been deserted or handed over as an infant and its mother's place had not been taken by a suitable substitute, it was for the child as though it had been deserted. Some children, whose mothers had deserted them at a later stage, still longed for them years after they had been taken into a public institution or foster-home: similarly in regard to their fathers, though here there was sometimes hostility, especially from boys. At least two boys whose fathers had been killed in the war when they were infants regarded this as if their fathers had deserted them on purpose. Clearly the real background was sometimes different from that which the child had created and believed in.

Then there were the children who had recently been removed from a neglectful and squalid home under a 'fit person' order. They were numerous and included many brothers and sisters taken away *en bloc* from their parents; the special 'problem families' considered later in this chapter were made up of such children and their parents.

The rest of the children came from families of all sizes and sorts, from homes with varying degrees of harmony and good nurture—or the reverse. Very few of the children had a background which seemed, by the criteria of common sense and psychiatry, wholly favourable.

(*a*) *Grouping of certain features of family and environment into three background patterns*. In order to bring some order into an enormous mass of social and psychological data, and to test the correctness of associations alleged to exist between backgrounds and behaviour, the relationships particularly studied in this series have been between disordered behaviour, on the one hand, and three main adverse influences, on the other. These three varieties of adverse influences may be summed up as: lack of parental affection ('rejection'); parental neglect; and a harsh repressive upbringing (see pp. 63–64). They are obviously not mutually exclusive. The reasons for singling them out are clinical experience and the evidence of such studies as that of Hewitt and Jenkins, who found correlation of the order of 0·5 to 0·7 between situational patterns mainly of this nature and behaviour patterns in maladjusted children.

The frequency with which individual items indicative of neglect, lack of parental affection, and harsh upbringing occurred in the 500 children (grouped according to the normality of their behaviour) is shown in Table 18. The children whose behaviour was only slightly abnormal are difficult to utilize, and attention will be chiefly concentrated on the relation between possible causal factors and the children whose behaviour was either normal or fell definitely into one of the three

Children's Behaviour

patterns—unsocialized aggressive, socialized delinquent, and over-inhibited neurotic.

(b) *Normal behaviour*. It is perhaps remarkable that 119, or more than a fifth of all the children admitted to a reception centre chiefly because they had no satisfactory home and background, nevertheless were normal in their behaviour and gave no grounds for inferring that psychological damage had been done. It is open to anyone to maintain that the children will in later years show disturbances as yet latent. But such speculations do not lend themselves readily to confirmation or disproof: so far as this investigation goes, follow-up findings reported in Chapter 5 lend no support to such fears.

Children who were deprived of their parents in the literal sense, and others deprived of the psychological advantages of parental love and care, nevertheless managed in a number of cases to preserve mental and social well-being. Over half of the children with normal behaviour came from exceptionally dirty and neglectful homes. The matter is considered later in this chapter under 'Effects of upbringing in a "problem family" '.

Eleven (9 per cent.) of the normal children had been in public care for a year or more, as against 20 per cent. of the children with abnormal behaviour. It cannot, however, be inferred from this that public care is more likely to conduce to abnormal behaviour. Indeed the main reason for admitting a child in public care into the Reception Centre was unsatisfactory behaviour; whereas the child received at the Centre direct from his home was admitted not so much because of his behaviour as of neglect by his parents. The eleven normally behaved children who had been in public care were received into the Centre because there were administrative reasons for reviewing their placement or because foster-mothers were no longer able to look after them.

2. CERTAIN BACKGROUND FEATURES RELATED TO THE CHILD'S RECENT BEHAVIOUR

The first need is to examine whether the data afford evidence of a significant association between, on the one hand, certain background features which may be adverse influences in the child's life and, on the other, the character of his recent behaviour. The influences studied were those listed in Table 18.

TABLE 18
CHILD'S CONDITION AT RECEPTION RELATED TO HOME AND UPBRINGING

Home and upbringing	CHILD'S CONDITION AT RECEPTION						Total No.
	Normal No.	(%)	Mildly disturbed No.	(%)	Definitely disturbed No.	(%)	
TOTALS	119	(23·8)	155	(31)	226	(45·2)	500
*1. Neglected by mother	81	(32·2)	87	(34·5)	84	(33·3)	252
*2. Mother lacking in affection	13	(9·3)	41	(29·3)	86	(61·4)	140
*3. Mother over-indulgent	4	(8)	13	(26)	33	(66)	50
4. Mother sexually loose	21	(23·3)	35	(38·9)	34	(37·8)	90
5. Mother in full-time employment	18	(22·8)	27	(34·2)	34	(43·0)	79
6. Mother physically handicapped	12	(23·1)	15	(28·8)	25	(48·1)	52
*7. Mother dull or defective	43	(36·1)	37	(31·1)	39	(32·8)	119
*8. Mother with other mental disability	37	(23·6)	37	(23·6)	83	(52·8)	157
*9. Neglected by father	61	(34·1)	50	(27·9)	68	(38·0)	179
10. Father lacking in affection	27	(19·6)	40	(29·0)	71	(51·4)	138
11. Father cruel and harsh	9	(20·5)	14	(31·8)	21	(47·7)	44
*12. Father over-indulgent	3	(9·7)	7	(22·6)	21	(67·7)	31
*13. Child separated from mother before 5 years old	32	(15·7)	76	(37·2)	96	(47·1)	204
14. Child illegitimate	29	(25·2)	38	(33·1)	48	(41·7)	115
*15. Child already in public care	11	(13·3)	30	(36·1)	42	(50·6)	83
*16. Mother long dead or unknown	10	(14·3)	29	(41·4)	31	(44·3)	70
17. Father long dead or unknown	22	(18·2)	43	(35·5)	56	(46·3)	121
18. Bad home atmosphere (discord)	41	(21·9)	60	(32·1)	86	(46·0)	187
*19. Home dirty	65	(43·3)	49	(32·7)	36	(24·0)	150

* Association statistically significant.

An association that was statistically significant at the 5 per cent. level was found to exist in respect of eleven items: maternal neglect, maternal lack of affection, maternal over-indulgence, maternal dullness or defect, other mental disability in the mother, paternal neglect, paternal over-indulgence, separation of the child from his mother before he was 5, public care of the child for at least six months (usually for several years) before

Children's Behaviour

reception, mother dead or unknown, and a dirty home. In some the association was highly significant.

The remarkably high proportion of children from dirty homes who were well adjusted in their mental condition (Table 19) has already been commented on, and to some extent reflects the predominantly extrinsic reasons for their reception as compared with the difficulties and troubles occasioned by the child himself which often determined the admission of the other children.

TABLE 19[1]

CHILD'S CONDITION AT RECEPTION RELATED TO STATE OF HOME*

State of home	CHILD'S CONDITION AT RECEPTION					
	Normal	Mildly disturbed	Definitely disturbed	χ^2	n	P
Home dirty	65	49	36	49·57	2	< 0·001
Home reasonably clean	43	76	148			

* Children already in public care excluded.

Much the same considerations apply in cases of neglect (Table 20), and it is permissible to conclude that a child may be neglected by his mother and live in dirty surroundings without suffering manifest psychological harm.

TABLE 20

CHILD'S CONDITION AT RECEPTION RELATED TO MOTHER'S SOLICITUDE*

Mother's solicitude	CHILD'S CONDITION AT RECEPTION					
	Normal	Mildly disturbed	Definitely disturbed	χ^2	n	P
Neglected by mother	81	87	84	36·14	2	< 0·001
Mother attentive	28	39	111			

*Children with mothers long dead or unknown excluded.

[1] The chi-square statistical test (χ^2) has been employed in these tables to determine how probable it is that the observed association between two variables could have been due merely to chance. When the probability of this (P) is small, the association between the variables is regarded as significant though not necessarily of a causal nature. It is commonly assumed that when P is greater than 0·05 the data are not sufficient to affirm any significant association.

The striking association between disturbance of behaviour and lack of maternal affection (Table 21) confirms the universal belief that if a child is deprived of his mother's love his mental well-being suffers.

TABLE 21

CHILD'S CONDITION AT RECEPTION RELATED TO MOTHER'S AFFECTION*

Mother's affection	CHILD'S CONDITION AT RECEPTION			χ^2	n	P
	Normal	Mildly disturbed	Definitely disturbed			
Mother lacking in affection	13	41	86	32·99	2	<0·001
Mother affectionate	96	85	109			

* Children with mothers long dead or unknown excluded.

The highly significant association shown in Table 22 may be taken as suggesting that a child who has been separated from his mother either temporarily or permanently before the age of 5 is more liable to disturbance of behaviour and personality than a child deprived of maternal care at a later age. The table includes 62 children who were under 5 on admission: 18 of these had been separated from their mothers ('permanently', i.e. for more than 2 years, or only temporarily); and 44 had not been away from their mothers up to the time of admission; 28 of these 62 children were 4 years old when received. The matter is discussed more fully later in this chapter (see p. 70).

TABLE 22

CHILD'S CONDITION AT RECEPTION RELATED TO SEPARATION FROM MOTHER BEFORE THE AGE OF 5 YEARS

Separation from mother	CHILD'S CONDITION AT RECEPTION			χ^2	n	P
	Normal	Mildly disturbed	Definitely disturbed			
Separated before 5 years	32	76	96	14·15	2	<0·001
Not separated before 5 years	87	79	130			

Children's Behaviour

The finding (Table 23) that normality of the child is fully compatible with dullness of the mother cannot be kept apart from the same finding in regard to maternal neglect. Many women of poor intelligence did not know how to care for their children's material needs; yet they were fond of their children and apparently satisfied their emotional needs. There was nothing in the children's behaviour that necessarily led to their being referred to the Centre, as was the case with so many children whose mothers were of average intelligence but lacking in other qualities that are probably more important for a a child's mental health.

TABLE 23

CHILD'S CONDITION AT RECEPTION RELATED TO MOTHER'S INTELLIGENCE*

Mother's intelligence	CHILD'S CONDITION AT RECEPTION					
	Normal	Mildly disturbed	Definitely disturbed	χ^2	n	P
Mother dull	43	37	39	13·47	2	0·001
Mother not dull	66	89	156			

* Children with mothers long dead or unknown excluded.

The association between psychopathic personality and neurotic disorder in the mother (psychotic disturbance in a few cases) on the one hand and disturbance in the child on the other (Table 24) is probably a causal relation (although it is less significant than that shown in the four preceding tables). It will be met again when the relation of these influences to a particular pattern of disturbed behaviour is being considered.

TABLE 24

CHILD'S CONDITION AT RECEPTION RELATED TO MOTHER'S MENTAL HEALTH

Mother's mental health	CHILD'S CONDITION AT RECEPTION					
	Normal	Mildly disturbed	Definitely disturbed	χ^2	n	P
Mother mentally unhealthy	37	37	83	6·16	2	0·047
Mother mentally healthy	72	89	112			

TABLE 25. CHILD'S CONDITION AT RECEPTION RELATED TO MOTHER'S INDULGENCE

Mother's indulgence	CHILD'S CONDITION AT RECEPTION					
	Normal	Mildly disturbed	Definitely disturbed	χ^2	n	P
Mother over-indulgent	4	13	33	12·25	2	0·003
Mother not over-indulgent	105	113	162			

TABLE 26. CHILD'S CONDITION AT RECEPTION RELATED TO FATHER'S SOLICITUDE*

Father's solicitude	CHILD'S CONDITION AT RECEPTION					
	Normal	Mildly disturbed	Definitely disturbed	χ^2	n	P
Neglected by father	61	50	68	13·41	2	<0·001
Father attentive	36	62	102			

* Children with fathers long dead or unknown excluded.

TABLE 27. CHILD'S CONDITION AT RECEPTION RELATED TO FATHER'S INDULGENCE

Father's indulgence	CHILD'S CONDITION AT RECEPTION					
	Normal	Mildly disturbed	Definitely disturbed	χ^2	n	P
Father over-indulgent	3	7	21	7·84	2	0·02
Father not over-indulgent	94	105	149			

TABLE 28. CHILD'S CONDITION AT RECEPTION RELATED TO PLACEMENT IN PUBLIC CARE BEFORE RECEPTION

Placement in public care	CHILD'S CONDITION AT RECEPTION					
	Normal	Mildly disturbed	Definitely disturbed	χ^2	n	P
In public care before reception	11	30	42	6·14	2	0·05
Not in public care before reception	108	125	184			

There is an evident link between over-indulgence of the mother and disturbed behaviour of the child (Table 25), but it would be imprudent to read a great deal into it. Over-indulgence is easy to conceal and extremely difficult to assess.

The negligent fathers were mostly the husbands of the negligent mothers already discussed, and the paradoxical finding shown in Table 26 probably calls for a similar explanation.

Over-indulgent fathers may be harmful to their children's well-being, if the association shown in Table 27 is a causal one, but no significant association between the father's harshness or lack of affection and disturbance in the child's psychological state could be discerned. In many cases, however, adequate information about the attitude and behaviour of the father was hard to obtain, and it would be contrary to common sense and experience if the lack of a demonstrably significant association between paternal affection and filial well-being in these families were accepted as a general truth.

As has been pointed out earlier in this chapter, many of the children coming to the Mersham Centre after they had been in the care of a public authority were admitted for the very reason that they were difficult. The association between behaviour and previous placement in public care (a not very significant one, as Table 28 shows) does not, therefore, warrant conclusions about the effect upon a child of being the ward of a public authority.

TABLE 29

CHILD'S CONDITION AT RECEPTION RELATED TO MOTHER'S AVAILABILITY

Mother's availability	CHILD'S CONDITION AT RECEPTION			χ^2	n	P
	Normal	Mildly disturbed	Definitely disturbed			
Mother dead or unknown	10	29	31	5·96	2	almost 0·05
Mother available	109	126	195			

The dubiously significant association between the presence of the mother and the behaviour of the child (Table 29) needs no comment. Many of the children acquired substitute mothers who brought them up with affection and care.

TABLE 30. CHILD'S PATTERN OF BEHAVIOUR AT RECEPTION RELATED TO HOME AND UPBRINGING

Home and upbringing	Normal	Un-socialized aggressive	Socialized delinquent	Inhibited, neurotic	Mixed	Slightly delinquent (socialized and un-socialized)	Slightly inhibited, neurotic	Total	Per cent.
	119	52	57	80	37	44	111	500	
1. Neglected by mother	81	15	25	35	9	18	69	252	50.4
*2. Mother lacking in affection	13	29	16	29	12	14	27	140	28
2a. Mother cruel or harsh	4	2	1	4	3	1	4	19	3.8
3. Mother over-indulgent	4	4	10	11	8	2	11	50	10
3a. Mother over-protective	1	2	3	7	3	1	5	22	4.4
4. Mother sexually loose	21	8	9	13	4	8	27	90	18
5. Mother in full-time employment	18	13	10	9	2	8	19	79	15.8
6. Mother physically handicapped	12	1	10	9	5	2	13	52	10
7. Mother dull or defective	43	4	11	15	9	10	27	119	23.8
*8. Mother with other mental disability	37	16	18	41	8	7	30	157	31.4
9. Child neglected by father	61	13	19	26	10	12	38	179	35.8
*10. Father lacking in affection	27	22	17	22	10	12	28	138	27.6
11. Father cruel or harsh	9	4	5	10	2	6	8	44	8.8
12. Father over-indulgent	3	2	8	5	6	2	5	31	6.2
12a. Father over-protective	..	..	1	1	1	..	..	3	0.6
13. Child separated from mother before 5 years of age	32	30	20	35	11	20	56	204	40.8
*14. Child illegitimate	29	17	8	15	8	7	31	115	23
*15. Child already in public care	11	14	4	18	6	12	18	83	16.6
16. Mother long dead or unknown	10	5	8	12	6	12	17	70	14
17. Father long dead or unknown	22	17	14	16	9	14	29	121	24.2
18. Bad home atmosphere (discord)	41	20	23	30	13	20	40	187	37.4
19. Home dirty	65	6	8	19	3	9	40	150	30

* Associations statistically significant.

3. CERTAIN BACKGROUND FEATURES RELATED TO CERTAIN PATTERNS OF DISTURBED BEHAVIOUR

The foregoing evidence on the association between certain unhappy background features in a child's life with his psychological condition on admission to the Reception Centre does not connect particular adverse influences with particular disorders of conduct. A further series of contingency tables was therefore drawn up and the heterogeneity of the patterns of behaviour in relation to these influences was examined by the χ^2 method.

Few statistically significant associations could be established or were expected; but in five instances, surprisingly, the figures suggested that the distribution of the children's behaviour patterns was not a random one when a particular influence had been at work (Table 30, items 2, 8, 10, 14, and 15). These statistically significant associations are shown in Tables 31 to 35.

The decidedly significant finding in Table 31 suggests that mothers who are unstable or mentally ill run a greater risk of generating neurotic disturbance than delinquency in their children. The welfare of the children may therefore be threatened if such mothers resume their upbringing, unless the mother's health has improved.

TABLE 31

CHILD'S PATTERN OF DISTURBED BEHAVIOUR AT RECEPTION RELATED TO MENTAL HEALTH OF MOTHER

	CHILD'S PATTERN OF DISTURBED BEHAVIOUR AT RECEPTION					
Mother's mental health	Unsocialized aggressive	Socialized delinquent	Inhibited, neurotic	χ^2	n	P
Mother mentally unhealthy	16	18	41	9·99	2	<0·01
Mother mentally healthy	31	31	27			

Lack of affection seems to favour the development of the 'unsocialized aggressive' type of behaviour in the child (Table 32). There is a significant difference between those who have an affectionate mother and those who have not.

TABLE 32
CHILD'S PATTERN OF DISTURBED BEHAVIOUR AT RECEPTION RELATED TO MOTHER'S AFFECTION*

Mother's affection	CHILD'S PATTERN OF DISTURBED BEHAVIOUR AT RECEPTION			χ^2	n	P
	Unsocialized aggressive	Socialized delinquent	Inhibited, neurotic			
Mother lacking in affection	29	16	29	8·46	2	<0·02
Mother affectionate	18	33	39			

* Children with mothers long dead or unknown excluded.

A significant difference is also apparent in Table 33. It suggests that a child whose father is lacking in affection inclines towards delinquency of an aggressive pattern.

TABLE 33
CHILD'S PATTERN OF DISTURBED BEHAVIOUR AT RECEPTION RELATED TO FATHER'S AFFECTION*

Father's affection	CHILD'S PATTERN OF DISTURBED BEHAVIOUR AT RECEPTION			χ^2	n	P
	Unsocialized aggressive	Socialized delinquent	Inhibited, neurotic			
Father lacking in affection	22	17	22	7·79	2	0·02
Father affectionate	13	26	42			

* Children with fathers long dead or unknown excluded.

TABLE 34
CHILD'S PATTERN OF DISTURBED BEHAVIOUR AT RECEPTION RELATED TO PLACEMENT IN PUBLIC CARE BEFORE RECEPTION

Placement in public care	CHILD'S PATTERN OF DISTURBED BEHAVIOUR AT RECEPTION			χ^2	n	P
	Unsocialized aggressive	Socialized delinquent	Inhibited, neurotic			
In public care before reception	14	4	18	8·07	2	<0·02
Not in public care before reception	38	53	62			

Children's Behaviour

There is a clear indication (Table 34) that children who were in public care are more likely to develop aggressive behaviour than other children.

The divergence between legitimate and illegitimate children is only just significant at the 5 per cent. level (Table 35); it

TABLE 35

CHILD'S PATTERN OF DISTURBED BEHAVIOUR AT RECEPTION RELATED TO LEGITIMACY

Legitimacy	CHILD'S PATTERN OF DISTURBED BEHAVIOUR AT RECEPTION					
	Unsocialized aggressive	Socialized delinquent	Inhibited neurotic	χ^2	n	P
Child illegitimate	17	8	15	} 6·16	2	0·05
Child legitimate.	35	49	65			

seems to be in the direction observed by Hewitt and Jenkins, who found that the illegitimate child inclines to unsocialized aggressive behaviour.

4. 'BACKGROUND PATTERNS' RELATED TO PATTERNS OF DISTURBED BEHAVIOUR

Before considering in greater detail the special issues (separation from the mother, and membership of a 'problem family') which have been emphasized of recent years, it is convenient to review here the clinical evidence bearing on a connexion between the pattern of abnormal behaviour in a child and the pattern of adverse influences, which may be called his harmful background. So far we have been examining not patterns but isolated items, the nineteen background features which might exert an adverse influence. Hewitt and Jenkins, in the investigation already alluded to, found a connexion, which they assumed to be causal, between background pattern and pattern of disturbed behaviour. The criteria they used were not fully applicable to the data here under consideration, but there is a broad agreement.

(*a*) *Definition of the background patterns.* Three background patterns were taken, which will be briefly, if perhaps misleadingly, called 'parental rejection' (lack of affection), 'neglect and bad company', and 'constraint' (harsh repressive upbringing).

'*Parental rejection*' was assumed whenever it was known that at least one of the first three conditions listed below, together with one or more of the remaining three conditions, had been fulfilled. These conditions were:

(1) Mother without affection for the child or showing dislike.
(2) Father without affection for the child or showing dislike.
(3) Child's birth unwanted and deplored.
(4) Child bereaved of parents through death or separated from them for a very long period (starting before he was 5 years old) as a result of desertion, illness, or official intervention.
(5) Child out of contact with parents since he passed into public care.
(6) Child unwanted or disliked by substitute-parents (i.e. stepmother or stepfather, relative acting as guardian, foster-parent).

'*Neglect and bad company*' was the pattern assumed when the first of the conditions listed below had been fulfilled together with at least one other. These conditions were:

(1) Exposure to the influence of delinquents, either the child's siblings or some of his associates in a poor or socially degraded neighbourhood.
(2) Living in a very dirty, ill-kept home.
(3) Lack of some of the necessities of life and decency because of parental neglect or incapacity.
(4) Lax or ill-timed discipline by an over-indulgent or sporadically harsh parent.

'*Constraint*' was assumed when at least two of the following conditions had been met:

(1) Rigid daily programme.
(2) Excessive discipline by parent or in a children's home or residential school.
(3) Domination and hyper-criticism by parent.
(4) Lack of warmth within family or group.
(5) Enforced isolation or social ostracism.
(6) Over-protection.

Children's Behaviour 65

A sharp classification was, of course, impracticable, if only because a child might well have passed from one of these situations to another (from, say, a neglectful home and criminal companions to a repressive atmosphere in a strictly organized residential school) and some would have come from homes which displayed very few or none of the defects listed. Nevertheless, it was in most cases possible to make a broad and on the whole satisfactory classification, after re-examining the full dossier of each child for this purpose. The most definite background pattern, and the most readily diagnosed, was that of 'parental rejection'.

It needs no emphasis that background patterns such as these cannot be held responsible for all the phenomena of disordered behaviour. As mentioned at the beginning of this chapter, hereditary predisposition, disease (e.g. epilepsy, with its effects upon personality and conduct), and a host of subtle influences, recent and remote, transient and permanent, co-operate to determine behaviour. Any relationship discovered between situation and behaviour must be partial.

In what follows the three 'background patterns' (parental rejection, neglect and bad company, and constraint) will be related to the 'behaviour patterns' (unsocialized aggression, socialized delinquency, and inhibited, neurotic behaviour) which were exhibited by the Mersham children. These behaviour patterns have been described in Chapter 3, where it was shown (Table 16) that of the 189 children concerned 52 showed unsocialized aggression, 57 showed socialized delinquency, and 80 showed inhibited, neurotic behaviour.

(*b*) *Background of 'parental rejection' related to 'unsocialized aggressive behaviour' in the child.* The link between a long-standing awareness of being unwanted and a tendency to be violent and antagonistic appeared fairly strong (Table 36). Besides the 39 'rejected' children in whom aggression was outstanding, 19 of the 23 'rejected' children with socialized delinquency showed some aggressive features also, as did 13 of the 27 with predominantly neurotic behaviour.

Much has been written by psychiatrists about the effects of maternal rejection, and a few have written about paternal rejection also; but, in spite of the elaborate psycho-analytic explanations offered, it is still impossible to discern in which

TABLE 36

CHILD'S PATTERN OF DISTURBED BEHAVIOUR AT RECEPTION RELATED TO 'REJECTION'

Background pattern	CHILD'S PATTERN OF DISTURBED BEHAVIOUR AT RECEPTION			χ^2	n	P
	Unsocialized aggressive	Socialized delinquent	Inhibited, neurotic			
Rejection .	39	23	27	23·01	2	<0·001
Acceptance .	13	34	53			

children parental rejection will lead to a disturbance of a particular sort. In very general terms it is obviously probable that a child who has found that his own parents do not want him and that he is being passed from reluctant hands to reluctant hands may feel that the world rejects him and that he is against the world.

(c) *Background of 'neglect and bad company' related to 'socialized delinquency' in the child.* Hewitt and Jenkins found a higher correlation (tetrachoric r 0·63±0·07) between these two than between any other background pattern and behaviour pattern. It is, however, questionable whether the use of tetrachoric r is here warranted, since it is unlikely that the regression is linear: at all events, the coexistence of two or more background patterns in the same child, and the succession of one such pattern upon another as the child's home and circumstances change, introduce so difficult and perhaps arbitrary an element into the dichotomy (which is based on qualitative unmeasured data) that it seemed best merely to calculate the frequency with which the 'neglect and bad company' pattern occurred in the background of the children showing a definite 'socialized delinquency' pattern of behaviour. Among the 57 children with socialized delinquency, 43 (75 per cent.) had been exposed to neglect and bad company (Table 38). There is, of course, some circularity here since a criterion of 'socialized delinquency' is that the child should have committed his offences with at least one companion (often his brother or sister), and exposure to delinquent company is likewise one of the criteria of 'neglect and bad company'. Since, however, other criteria which do not overlap enter into the respective assessments, this partial circularity does not nullify the striking frequency with which the particular background has preceded the particular pattern of behaviour.

A sharp distinction between background patterns would conceal in these 'socialized delinquents' the way in which one sort of background apparently brings about a change in the child which may favour his resorting to bad company which in turn influences his behaviour. There were, for example, sixteen children who had been stealing or wandering away in company with other children ('socialized delinquency') and who also were destructive, defiant, and prone to outbursts of temper. The aggressive traits had presumably appeared first in response to the dislike and 'rejection' which the children experienced from their parents and others. The mother of such a child, for example, would often have told him to 'clear off out of her sight' wherever he liked to go in their sordid neighbourhood; or the child, deprived of any welcome or affection in his home, had sought solace among the members of some juvenile gang. Through some such chain of events many of the children in this little group had come to pilfer and wander about so that this became, after a while, the habitual pattern of behaviour.

(*d*) *Background of 'constraint' related to 'neurotic behaviour' in the child.* Here also it is hardly appropriate to attempt to derive too much from data about the child's background which amount to a broad inference, often modified by another coexistent or previous pattern, less prominent or recent than the main one.

Fifty of the 80 children showing the 'neurotic' pattern of behaviour had been exposed to a 'repressive' regimen, lacking warmth or flexibility (Table 37). If the children were then subdivided into those who avoided company through morbid shyness (47) and those who, though anxious and otherwise neurotic, were companionable (33), the 'constraint' background was found in 75 per cent. of the former, but in only 45 per cent. of the latter.

The association between 'constraint' and inhibited neurotic behaviour is evidently not fortuitous.

In some of these children, as in the delinquent group, more than one sort of background could, of course, be discerned, and this had not come about fortuitously. For example, a child's parents had not wanted her, and, after a period of rejection and neglect during which she consorted with dubious or criminal people, she had been taken into care and sent to a large children's home. This is a rather extreme instance, but there were many who showed combinations of circumstances which

TABLE 37

CHILD'S PATTERN OF DISTURBED BEHAVIOUR AT RECEPTION RELATED TO 'CONSTRAINT'

Background pattern	CHILD'S PATTERN OF DISTURBED BEHAVIOUR AT RECEPTION					
	Unsocialized aggressive	Socialized delinquent	Inhibited neurotic	χ^2	n	P
Constraint	28	21	50	8·73	2	<0·02
No constraint	24	36	30			

could similarly be accounted for, and in these children a corresponding mixture of types of behaviour was manifest. Violent and aggressive features bespoke the hostility or aversion of the child's parents, or his earlier delinquent acts attested undesirable associates and neglectful parents. The neglect by the parents was sometimes in part the consequence of their physical ailments or of their mental deficiencies.

The 80 children comprised in the neurotic group had fairly numerous physical and mental disabilities. One had epilepsy, 6 had chronic physical illnesses, 2 had had severe illnesses in infancy, 7 were mentally dull, 4 had severe quasi-psychotic disturbances. Though these conditions cannot be regarded as forming part of the children's external background, they had evidently led to a restriction of their lives, and had evoked reactions to attitudes of adults, schoolmates, and playmates which had conduced to the development of neurotic symptoms.

A comparison of the incidence of the three background patterns in the children exhibiting the three patterns of disturbed behaviour is given in Table 38. Many of the children had, of course, more than one background pattern.

(e) *Mixed patterns and 'sibling rivalry'.* The 37 children who showed severe disturbances of behaviour (Table 16, p. 44) that could not be fitted to any one of the three patterns but contained fairly equally balanced components of two or all of these, might have been expected to show a corresponding diversity and intensity of background patterns. But this was not the case. 'Rejection' was the main background pattern in 13 of them, 'neglect and bad company' in 9, and 'constraint' in 11. Two

TABLE 38

CHILD'S PATTERN OF DISTURBED BEHAVIOUR AT RECEPTION RELATED TO BACKGROUND PATTERN

Background pattern	CHILD'S PATTERN OF DISTURBED BEHAVIOUR AT RECEPTION			
	Unsocialized aggression (52 children)	Socialized delinquency (57 children)	Inhibited, neurotic (80 children)	TOTAL
Rejection	39	23	27	89
Neglect and bad company	5	43	5	53
Constraint	28	21	50	99

or three of these background patterns seldom coexisted: of the 13 'rejected', for example, only 3 had also been exposed to neglect and bad company. A remarkable feature of this group of children, however, was their quarrelsomeness: they were constantly at war with the other children, to an extent that made it difficult to place them anywhere except in a childless foster-home, and even then school became a battleground. Twenty-four of the 37 children showed this trait conspicuously: 7 came from large poverty-stricken families, in which they had had to compete with their brothers and sisters for an overburdened mother's attention. The parents of 6 had shown open preference for another child, and 4 children had step-parents with children of their own. What has been called 'sibling rivalry' had therefore operated powerfully on these children, apparently producing antagonism towards most other children: they had come directly from their homes to Mersham with this pattern of behaviour already formed.

5. EFFECTS OF SEPARATION FROM MOTHER

It has lately been maintained, chiefly on the strength of various English and American investigations, that 'prolonged separation of a child from his mother (or mother-substitute) during the first five years of life stands foremost among the causes of delinquent character development'[1] and that upbringing in an institution during early life is very injurious to the growth of personality, leading to 'aggressive, distractible, uncontrolled behaviour. Normal patterns of anxiety and self-inhibition are not developed. Human identifications are limited, and relationships are weak and easily broken . . .'[2] If these views are correct, the children in this series who suffered such privation of maternal love should have shown a high prevalence of disturbed conduct of the sort described and should have included few whose conduct either was normal or bore the imprint of overt anxiety, without aggression or delinquency. It has already been shown in this chapter (Tables 28 and 29) that a comparison of those children who had been apart from their mothers before the age of 5 (irrespective of whether the separation was lasting or temporary) with those who had not, reveals a significant difference in their condition when they came to the Centre.

(*a*) *Evidence connecting separation with disturbed behaviour.* 'Temporary' separation means physical separation of the child from his mother for a period of not less than three months and not more than two years. In a few instances children had been, from their early months, in the care of adoptive mothers, or foster-mothers who were to all intents and purposes mother-substitutes: these women were therefore counted as mothers in this particular context. 'Lasting' separation means continuous physical separation of the child from the mother for more than two years immediately before admission to the Reception Centre. The majority of the children in this group had been away from their mothers for most of their lives, and some had been in institutions from the time of weaning.

As varying periods had elapsed from the time of separation to the time of admission to the Centre, the figures for children temporarily or permanently separated from their mothers at various age-periods (Table 39) can be used only with some reservation in judging the effect of separation upon the children. Moreover, in such a small population due allowance could not

[1] J. Bowlby, 'Forty-four Juvenile Thieves, their Characteristics and Home Life', *Int. J. Psycho.-Anal.*, London, 1944, **25**, 19.
[2] W. Goldfarb, *Amer. J. Orthopsychiat.*, 1949, **19**, 624.

be made for the children who were still under 5 when admitted to the Centre and who, therefore, could hardly as yet be regarded as lastingly separated between 2 and 5 or as separated after the age of 5. The extent of this minor complication may be gauged from the following facts. Of the 500 children received 62 were under the age of 5 years, and 18 of these had at some time been separated from their mothers for more than 3 months.

TABLE 39

CHILD'S BEHAVIOUR AT RECEPTION RELATED TO SEPARATION FROM MOTHER AT VARIOUS AGES

	CHILD'S BEHAVIOUR			
Separation of child from mother	Normal	Mildly disturbed	Definitely disturbed	TOTAL
	119	155	226	500
Temporary separation before the age of 2 years	4	12	12	28
Lasting separation before the age of 2 years	6	23	25	54
Temporary separation between ages of 2 and 5 years	9	21	38	68
Lasting separation between ages of 2 and 5 years	13	20	21	54
Temporary separation after age of 5 years	18	28	32	78
Lasting separation after age of 5 years	4	10	20	34
TOTAL	54	114	148	316

So far as the mental condition of these 18 young children could be assessed, 8 seemed quite normal, 8 had minor disturbances, and 2 were aggressive and spiteful boys of 4½ (one had been abandoned by his mother at the age of 2, and the other had been in a series of foster-homes from the age of 5 months, though his mother had visited him regularly).

When each of the varieties of separation shown in Table 39 is examined, it is only lasting separation which began before the age of 2 that shows a statistically significant difference in behaviour between those separated and those not separated, and it is the mildly rather than the definitely disturbed group that makes the chief contribution to the χ^2 (Table 40 (a)). The significance of the association is much more pronounced when, instead of comparing those permanently separated before the age of 2 (54) with all other children in the series (446), they are compared only with those (184) who had not been exposed to lasting separation from their mother at any age (Table 40 (b)). This is not surprising. Two of the main reasons for children being separated from their mothers after the age of 2 are lack

TABLE 40

CHILD'S BEHAVIOUR AT RECEPTION RELATED TO (a) LASTING SEPARATION FROM MOTHER BEFORE THE AGE OF TWO YEARS, (b) NO SEPARATION AT ANY AGE

	Separation of child from mother	BEHAVIOUR AT TIME OF RECEPTION			χ^2	n	P
		Normal	Mildly disturbed	Definitely disturbed			
(a)	Lasting separation before age of 2 years	6	23	25	6·72	2	0·04
	No lasting separation before age of 2 years	113	132	201			
(b)	Lasting separation before age of 2 years	6	23	25	14·7	2	<0·001
	No separation at any age	65	41	78			

of affection on the part of the mother and abnormalities of behaviour, such as delinquency, on the part of the child. Since all these children have been excluded from the 'control' or contrasted group in Table 40 (b), the 184 who remain include a large contingent of the 'problem family' children many of whom (as will be shown later) are well-adjusted psychologically, and a few children whose admission to the Centre had only been caused by a temporary family upheaval such as the illness of a parent. The differences between such children and the fifty-four orphaned and rejected children who were separated from their mothers before they were 2 years old must inevitably be considerable and cannot be attributed to the effects of separation alone. There was no other significant

Children's Behaviour

association of the child's mental state with temporary or lasting separation from the mother, though that with temporary separation between the ages of 2 and 5 years is suggestive ($\chi^2 = 5\cdot67$, $n = 2$, $P = 0\cdot06$).

Although temporary separation from the mother can have a disturbing effect upon a child (especially if he has not been adequately prepared for it), it is prolonged separation from the mother which chiefly calls for further notice. Among our 500 children 142 had suffered such lasting separation from their mothers: 54 before the age of 2 years, 54 at ages between 2 and 5 years, and 34 after the age of 5 (Table 39, last column). Twenty-three of these children, among them 6 who had been separated from their mothers before the age of 2, showed no abnormality of behaviour (Table 39, first column), and this apparent absence of ill-effects calls for closer scrutiny. The sixty-six 'definitely disturbed' children (Table 39, third column) also need to be considered in greater detail to compare their behaviour with the descriptions by other investigators of 'institutional' children and children separated from their mothers early in life.

Many of the fifty-four children with normal behaviour had found other persons to stand in their mothers' stead, but not all had been so fortunate. One girl, for instance, had passed at an age of less than 2 years into the hands of a woman who was indifferent to her. Another had been shown actual dislike by her foster-mother. A third child had been deserted by her mother at the age of a few months and had then lived with several relatives none of whom had wanted her, yet apparently she had not suffered thereby. In general, however, it was characteristic for the children in this group that they had successfully taken to women who had assumed their mothers' role in caring for them. This applied to 3 of the 6 normal children permanently separated from their mothers before the age of 2 as compared with only 5 of the 25 'definitely disturbed' children in this group. The other three children with normal behaviour had spent their lives in institutions, where two of them had had good mother-substitutes, but it is not clear why the third child was free from the alleged consequences of institutional upbringing.

General statements that early separation from their mothers and institutional upbringing exert a specific adverse effect on children, therefore, need to be qualified.[1] Striking generalizations may have the advantage of arousing interest in this important subject, but they can mislead: an appreciable proportion (17 per cent.) of the 108 children in this series who were separated permanently from their mothers below the age of 5 did not show abnormal behaviour later in their childhood, even if they had been brought up in public institutions.

The most illuminating examples are the 11 children in this group whose behaviour was normal although they had been separated from both parents before the age of 5. None of these children had been wanted or loved by their parents: the mothers of 2 had died and their fathers were unknown; 4 had been deserted by both parents; and 5 had been neglected or disliked by their mothers and, with the exception of two, also by their fathers. Five of these 11 children had spent the greater part of their lives in institutions.

The illegitimate daughter of a mother who died insane came into public care shortly after birth and had many changes of nursery. At the age of 10 she was placed in a foster-home, and, after further changes, she came to the Mersham Reception Centre as an adolescent. Her conduct was normal; continued observation and psychiatric examination showed neither neurotic nor delinquent traits. She was an attractive, sociable girl, interested in other people, adaptable and betraying only in her preference for group life the unusual circumstances of her upbringing.

Three of the 11 normal children had been placed with foster-parents, but only one before the age of 3.

A boy who had been abandoned at the age of 2 was placed with affectionate foster-parents within a year. They looked after him until he was 8, when he was moved to another home for a time. After he had been in the Reception Centre he returned to his first foster-parents, and has since been happy and contented.

Another child of this group who was illegitimate lost her mother at the age of 4. She was then placed with a family, but both the foster-father and his son disliked her and showed it; her maternal grandparents, however, kept in touch with her and were much attached to her.

Two other girls, sisters, had been deserted by their mother seven years previously; they were then placed in a number of children's

[1] Judgements of personality based on Rorschach and other tests, or on psychoanalytical interpretation, do not come within the purview of this study.

homes and foster-homes. A year before they were admitted to the Reception Centre they had been returned to the care of their father. The father, who was in an early stage of mental illness, made sexual assaults upon them. In spite of their troubled background, the girls seemed well adjusted and of good personality and conduct.

The need to qualify any general indictment of institutional upbringing would be more obvious in a study based on a less selected population than that of the Mersham Centre. Children of normal personality who were doing well in either foster-homes or institutions were only infrequently referred to the Centre.

What applies to institutional upbringing also applies to maternal deprivation. Unduly dogmatic statements about ill-effects of maternal deprivation often leave out of account the emotional hazards and harms children may suffer from bad mothers and indifferent mother-substitutes, or the variety of sources (including the father) from whom children may draw the love and support necessary for their happiness. It is better to be cautious and to stress the need for attention 'not only to ages and periods of deprivation, but also to the quality of the child's relation to his mother before deprivation, his experiences with mother-substitutes, if any, during separation, and the reception he gets from his mother or foster-mother when at last he becomes settled again'.[1] These, however, do not by any means exhaust the matters to which sober research into this question must be addressed.

There remains to be considered the alleged specific connexion between a child's separation from his mother in his early years and the development of a characteristic affectionless character, associated with delinquency. It is necessary for this purpose, to turn from the children with normal behaviour to those with abnormalities.

In the classification here employed, the findings (Table 41) indicate no clear connexion between separation from the mother in early childhood and any particular variety of disturbed behaviour. The children in the two definitely delinquent groups taken together exceed the definitely neurotic inhibited groups; but the balance is redressed if the slightly delinquent

[1] J. Bowlby, *Maternal Care and Mental Health*, W.H.O., Geneva, 1951, p. 48.

TABLE 41
CHILD'S PATTERN OF DISTURBED BEHAVIOUR RELATED TO SEPARATION FROM MOTHER AT VARIOUS AGES*

Separation of child from mother	Unsocialized aggression	Socialized delinquency	Inhibited, neurotic	Mixed	Slightly delinquent	Slightly inhibited, neurotic	TOTAL
Temporary separation before the age of 2 .	7	3	2	..	4	8	24
Lasting separation before the age of 2 .	7	5	8	5	8	15	48
Temporary separation between the age of 2 and 5 . . .	9	8	17	4	4	17	59
Lasting separation between the age of 2 and 5 . . .	7	4	8	2	4	16	41
Temporary separation after the age of 5 .	5	9	13	5	9	19	60
Lasting separation after the age of 5 .	4	4	9	3	6	4	30
TOTAL . . .	39 (14)	33 (9)	57 (16)	19 (7)	35 (12)	79 (31)	262 (89)

* Lasting separation before the age of 5 in brackets.

are set against the slightly neurotic. In the scarcely significant association shown in Table 42, the trend is for the children separated from their mothers to fall into the aggressive group rather than into the group of socialized delinquents among whom most of the juvenile thieves were to be found: so far as definite neurotic disturbances are concerned, the children separated from their mothers tend to behave like the other children. The figures as a whole, while too small to permit a clear

TABLE 42
CHILD'S PATTERN OF DISTURBED BEHAVIOUR AT RECEPTION RELATED TO SEPARATION FROM MOTHER BEFORE THE AGE OF 5 YEARS

	PATTERN OF DEFINITELY DISTURBED BEHAVIOUR					
Separation	Unsocialized aggressive	Socialized delinquent	Inhibited neurotic	χ^2	n	P
Lasting or temporary separation before the age of 5 years .	30	20	35	5.7	2	0.06
Not separated before the age of 5 years . .	22	37	45			

inference, fail to confirm the belief that a characteristic form of delinquent personality, recognizable on psychiatric examination, commonly ensues upon a child's separation from his mother in his early years.

(*b*) *Affective coldness and delinquency.* To check this supposed relationship further, the records of those children were studied whose behaviour before and after admission and while at the Centre indicated that their affective response was cold to an abnormal degree, so that they could be described as showing the affectionless character that is pronounced in some delinquents. There were 19 such children. They comprise 10 out of the 184 who had never been separated from their mothers for more than a few weeks; 4 out of the 174 who had been separated only temporarily, and 5 out of the 142 who had suffered prolonged separation from their mothers, though in only one instance from before the age of 2 years. Affective coldness cannot therefore be shown to be either a frequent outcome of separation or an outcome only of separation in the Mersham group. The data, indeed, show no statistically significant association with the length or stage of the period of separation ($\chi^2 = 4\cdot 03$, $n = 2$, $P > 0\cdot 05$).

These findings do nothing to cast doubt on the immense value to a child of enjoying his mother's love and care—a matter on which the majority of mankind has long been agreed; but they suggest that the relationship of cause to effect is here intricate and not yet ready to be cast into a form which he who runs may read.

6. EFFECTS OF UPBRINGING IN A 'PROBLEM FAMILY'

Much attention has been concentrated during the last few years upon 'problem families' in which the children are neglected and the normal decencies of a home ignored. The squalor, the lack of regard for order and seemly conduct, the failure to give thought or effort to care of the children horrify those who are new to such conditions, while at the same time provoking wonder in these observers when they find that the children in such homes are sometimes happy. Since slums are commonly held to breed crime, and mental health is more readily expected in the offspring of self-respecting than of shiftless and degraded parents, the actual condition of the children removed to the Reception Centre from homes in which neglect and squalor prevailed deserves separate study.

There were in this series 66 'problem families', i.e. families known to the children's officer or the National Society for the Prevention of Cruelty to Children because of child-neglect, dirt, and squalor. From these 66 families, 141 children were received into the Centre; in some instances only one child from a large family was referred.

(a) *The family characteristics.* The characteristics of these families can be briefly stated. They were of low social class, 18 per cent. falling into the Registrar General's social class III, 4 per cent. into social class IV, and 73 per cent. into social class V; three families could not be classified (cf. Table 5, p. 19).

The average size of the 'problem families' was larger than that of families in the general population, or of the other families represented by children at the Centre; but the family income did not differ materially from that of the other Mersham Centre families (cf. Table 43 with Table 7, p. 21).

TABLE 43

'PROBLEM FAMILIES': FAMILY INCOME RELATED TO FAMILY SIZE

Family income	'PROBLEM FAMILIES' WITH						TOTAL
	Only child	2 children	3 children	4 children	5 children	6 or more children	
Under £3 a week	..	1	1	..	1	5	8
£3–£5 a week .	..	3	5	7	2	4	21
Over £5 a week	1	2	2	3	4	18	30
Nil or unknown	1	..	2	1	1	2	7
TOTAL . .	2	6	10	11	8	29	66

Many fathers in the 'problem families' were unemployed (23 out of 51 who were alive and known); 7 others had only casual work: less than half had regular work. Three only of these families were motherless; in 15, however, the father had died or deserted the family. The two parents in 31 of the families were on bad terms with each other, creating an atmosphere of discord and ill will, and in only 6 was there genuine harmony between the parents. Eleven of the fathers were cruel and brutal to their wives and children, and 3 of the wives had sometimes attacked their husbands violently: cruelty to the children was less common, occurring in only 5 families. Four of the fathers and 2 of the mothers had been in jail, mostly for larceny. A quarter of the fathers were often drunk, and of the mothers nearly a third (19) were sexually loose, engaging in casual affairs or repeatedly leaving their husbands to live with other men.

The mental qualities of the parents were on the whole decidedly poor: a quarter of the fathers, and half of the mothers, were below average in intelligence, 6 being certified defectives; and a fifth of the fathers and just over a quarter of the mothers were neurotic, psychopathic, or psychotic. In all, 32 of the 54 fathers on whom information was available, and 50 of 64 mothers, were handicapped by significant mental or physical disabilities (including inferior intelligence). In at least 28 families both parents had some medical disability: as a rule both father and mother were dull or psychopathic.

TABLE 44

'PROBLEM FAMILIES': DISABILITIES OF BOTH PARENTS IN 28 FAMILIES

Mothers with		DISABILITIES IN THE CORRESPONDING FATHERS			
		Physical	Mental defect or dullness	Psychotic	Psychopathic personality
Physical disability	2	1	1	..	..
Mental defect or dullness	18	3	11	..	4
Neurosis	4	..	..	..	4
Psychosis	1	..	1	..	..
Psychopathic personality	3	1	1	1	..
	28	5	14	1	8

The picture presented by the prolific parents of these 'problem families'—so often shiftless, dull, psychopathic, discordant, and out of work—conforms to what previous investigators have found and described in vivid language.

(b) *The children: characteristics and behaviour.* Most of the 141 children of these 66 'problem families' who were sent to the Centre were admitted together with their brothers and sisters: only 30 came unaccompanied, and these single admissions had usually come about because the particular child had shown uncontrollable behaviour. As a rule the whole sibship had been removed, excepting babies and adolescents who were already in employment.

The level of intelligence among the 141 children was unsatisfactory. Four per cent. had an intelligence quotient below 70 on the Stanford-Binet test, 30 per cent. were between 70 and 89, 49 per cent. between 90 and 109, 12 per cent. between 110 and 129, and 5 per cent. over 130. Though the results of a single intelligence test, such as the revised Stanford-Binet, cannot be taken without reserve, it seems clear that there is an unduly high proportion of dull children here. Their personality and behaviour, however, were in pleasing contrast to their intelligence: 66 of them were quite normal, and 46 showed only slight evidences of delinquency or neurosis. Of the 29 who were decidedly disturbed in conduct, a majority (17) showed anxiety and other neurotic symptoms. The neurotic reactions were understandable from the social isolation, mortification, and, occasionally, harsh treatment to which the children in question had been exposed. Moreover, (Table 45) the children who came to the Centre in a family group were less disturbed than those who came alone.

TABLE 45

'PROBLEM FAMILIES': BEHAVIOUR OF CHILDREN ADMITTED ALONE OR WITH SIBLINGS

Children		Normal	Mildly delinquent	Mildly neurotic	Unsocialized aggressive	Socialized delinquent	Inhibited neurotic	Mixed
Unaccompanied by sibs . .	30	8	1	7	3	3	6	2
Accompanied by sibs . .	111	58	8	30	1	2	11	1
TOTAL . .	141	66	9	37	4	5	17	3

The proportion of children undisturbed in behaviour is considerably higher in the 'problem families' than in the general run of children admitted to the Centre (Table 46).

An impressive demonstration of the normality of many children from 'problem families' was the speed with which, after years of drift and dirt, they fell in with the more civilized way of life at the Centre. Some of the older children were surprisingly mature and responsible; though intellectually and educationally below the average, they showed practical sense and even resourcefulness, caring for their younger brothers and sisters and sometimes actually stepping into a protective, succouring role towards their feckless parents, e.g. using their pocket-money to buy cigarettes and other needs or luxuries for the mother and father. This family cohesion and loyalty was often striking, and many of the children were deeply resentful at having been taken away from their homes by order of the court.

TABLE 46

BEHAVIOUR OF CHILDREN FROM 'PROBLEM FAMILIES' AND OF OTHER CHILDREN AT RECEPTION

Behaviour of children	141 'problem family' children		359 other children	
	Number	Per cent.	Number	Per cent.
Normal	66	47	51	14
Near normal	46	33	113	32
Abnormal	29	20	195	54

TABLE 47

ATTITUDE OF PARENTS TO CHILDREN ADMITTED TO THE CENTRE. 'PROBLEM FAMILIES' AND OTHER FAMILIES*

Children	Lacking mother's affection	Deserted or bereaved of mother	Treated harshly by mother	Over-indulged by mother	Lacking father's affection	Deserted or bereaved of father	Treated harshly by father	Over-indulged by father
141 children from 'problem families'	26 (18)	7 (5)	4 (3)	3 (2)	45 (32)	7 (5)	11 (8)	3 (2)
359 other children	115 (32)	67 (19)	15 (4)	47 (13)	94 (26)	102 (28)	34 (9)	28 (8)

* Percentages in brackets.

(c) *Parental attitudes and behaviour*. The attitude of the parents in these families varied enormously; but a majority, especially of the mothers, were fond of the children whose material needs and social training they neglected, often through ineptness. Only 26 children, i.e. 18 per cent., had mothers who were lacking in affection towards them (Table 47), and 7 more had been deprived in early childhood of their mothers through death or desertion. The other features of their background are set against the background of other children admitted to the Centre in Table 48.

TABLE 48

MISCONDUCT OF PARENTS: 'PROBLEM FAMILIES' AND OTHER FAMILIES

Children	Mother sexually loose	Mother with criminal record	Mother alcoholic	Details of mother's conduct unknown	Father criminal	Father quarrelsome with mother	Father cruel to mother	Father alcoholic	Details of father's conduct unknown
141 children from 'problem families'	36 (26)	2 (1)	2 (1)	1 (1)	5 (4)	66 (47)	34 (24)	29 (21)	24 (17)
359 other children	54 (15)	14 (4)	8 (2)	39 (11)	24 (7)	120 (33)	40 (11)	30 (8)	87 (24)

On the favourable side of the balance for the 'problem families' is the greater proportion of affectionate mothers; on the unfavourable side are the mothers more prone to sexual laxity, the fathers more prone to cruelty, quarrelsomeness, and excessive drinking. The history of these children after they had left Mersham is considered in the next chapter.

SUMMARY

A. ASSOCIATION BETWEEN DETAILS OF CHILDREN'S PREVIOUS LIVES AND THEIR MENTAL HEALTH ON ADMISSION

1. Nineteen features of each child's parental and personal background were analysed to discover a relation between them and the normality or otherwise of his mental state when admitted to the Centre.

2. Eleven features showed a significant association with mental health. They were: maternal neglect, lack of maternal affection, maternal over-indulgence, maternal dullness or mental defect, maternal insanity or other psychopathy, paternal neglect, paternal over-indulgence, separation of child from mother before the age of 5, prolonged public care, and a dirty home. These features partly overlap.

3. The associations were not always in the direction which might have been expected. The group of children from very dirty homes included a higher proportion whose mental state was normal than

Children's Behaviour

was found in children from clean homes. A similar disparity, in favour of neglected children, was evident when children whose mothers had grossly neglected them were compared with those who had attentive mothers. The disparity between children whose mothers were intellectually dull or defective and the others was of the same order.

B. ASSOCIATION BETWEEN DETAILS OF CHILDREN'S PREVIOUS LIVES AND THE PATTERN OF THEIR DISTURBED BEHAVIOUR

4. A separate analysis was made to determine whether certain features of the child's background were specifically associated with particular patterns of disturbed behaviour.

5. Five background features showed a statistically significant association with patterns of disturbed behaviour. They were: mother neurotic or psychopathic; mother lacking in affection for child; father lacking in affection for child; prolonged stay in public care; illegitimacy.

6. A mentally unhealthy mother tended to produce a neurotic reaction in the child; if mother or father were not affectionate, or if the child had been in public care, unsocialized aggressive behaviour was more likely to have developed.

C. ASSOCIATION BETWEEN ADVERSE SITUATIONS IN THE CHILDREN'S HOME AND UPBRINGING, AND THEIR PATTERNS OF DISTURBED BEHAVIOUR

7. Three broad situations were defined, as objectively as possible. They were: parental rejection of the child; neglect and bad company; constraint. They were considerably broader than the background details dealt with in the preceding section, but took account of these.

8. Parental rejection was found to be significantly related to unsocialized aggression in the child. Neglect and bad company had often preceded socialized delinquency, and the constraint of a repressive regimen had been imposed on nearly two-thirds of the neurotic children.

9. *Separation.* Unless separation of child from mother had occurred before the age of 2 years and had been lasting, it bore no statistically significant relation to the normality or otherwise of the child's mental state at the time of admission. No clear connexion was evident between separation from the mother and a particular pattern of disturbed behaviour. Neither delinquency nor incapacity for affectionate relationships was significantly more frequent in the separated children.

10. All children who showed an 'affectionless character' were reviewed: there were nineteen of them. Ten of them had never been separated from their mothers for more than a few weeks; five had suffered prolonged separation, but in only one child had this begun before he was 2 years old.

11. *'Problem families.'* Sixty-six 'problem families', characterized by gross neglect and squalor, were represented in the sample; they accounted for 141 children. Relations between the parents were unsatisfactory in all but six of the families, and many of the parents were mentally handicapped in personality or intelligence. The mothers, however, were affectionate to their children. Collectively the children were of lower intelligence, though freer from delinquency or neurosis, than the rest of the Mersham children.

5
Subsequent Histories: Outcome

I. INTRODUCTORY

(a) *Questions raised.* An integral part of this study has been the inquiry into what happened to the children—and what happened in the children—after they had left the Reception Centre at Mersham. The follow-up could cover a period of three years at most: it could not include a close study of the child's mental state at the end of this time; and it had to rely in part on written information, unavoidably subjective, from many people with differing standards and outlook. Inference must be cautious, but nevertheless some instructive conclusions may be drawn.

Two main questions are raised: what good—or what harm—has the stay in the Reception Centre done the child? and what factors determine the course of his further development and behaviour? To answer the first question, we should have some notion of what would have happened to the child if no action had been taken and he had been left at home. To answer the second question, which is a prerequisite for answering the first, surmises are unavoidable. It is impossible to know what a child's future would have been in hypothetical circumstances if we do not know which circumstances will particularly affect him and what his response to them will be. A study such as is here reported cannot provide a satisfactory answer to fundamental questions of cause and effect in human behaviour. Many experiments and advances in knowledge will be necessary before that remote goal is reached. But an incomplete survey can still show whether children's behaviour and well-being are better after they have been at a Reception Centre than before, and can throw some light on the trustworthiness of the social and medical beliefs which guide us in what we do for 'deprived' children.

(b) *Personal visits compared with postal inquiries.* After they had left Mersham, inquiries were made about the children at the end of the first and the second year. A letter was sent to the welfare officer or other responsible person, drawing attention to what action had been recommended at the Centre and asking whether this had been carried out and what was the child's progress and present condition. The replies to these postal

86 *Subsequent Histories: Outcome*

inquiries were in the main full and informative; some were supplemented by progress reports from welfare officers, the children's officer, psychiatric social workers, and others who had visited the child or received official information about his placement and progress.

Reports so obtained are less valuable than those collected by a trained investigator who makes direct inquiries on the spot and also interviews the child. Because of the formidable practical difficulties, it was not possible to make such personal inquiries of all the children. It was decided to carry them out on 100 children, 50 boys and 50 girls consecutively admitted to the Centre at least two years before: if in these children, on whom the postal inquiries described above had been made as a routine, detailed examination by social worker and psychiatrist revealed a different state of affairs from what had apparently been shown in the postal inquiry, the findings of the latter could hardly be utilized; if they tallied, a larger sample of the children could be included in the study of outcome than if it were restricted to the 100 children of the special inquiry.

2. PERSONAL VISITS

(*a*) *Selection of sample.* The sample consisted of children admitted between April and December 1948 (eight months). Exceptions to the consecutive inclusions were children placed in boarding-schools or hostels too far away to be visited: for these were substituted the next consecutive admissions of children who were still living in the county of Kent or within fifty miles of London. Eighteen children were thus excluded, most of whom had been referred by the court and who were delinquent or neurotic. Concerning 14 of these, postal inquiries had yielded replies: 2 were well adjusted and happy, 5 fairly well adjusted, and 7 had not done well; these reports indicated a great improvement in the behaviour of 2 children, some improvement in 5, and stand-still or deterioration in 7. On the other four who had left Kent, postal reports after one year were received, but after two years they could not be traced.

(*b*) *Procedure: social investigation.* A visit was paid by the psychiatric social worker (Miss Woods) to the place where each of the children lived—foster-home, children's home or residential school—except for three children whom I visited in

Subsequent Histories: Outcome

approved schools. When visiting a foster-home the psychiatric social worker was accompanied by the responsible welfare officer, who was in touch with the family and well informed about the conditions in the home, the personality of the foster-mother, and other circumstances affecting the child's well-being.

The psychiatric social worker collected and recorded systematically data about the conditions prevailing in the home and about the child's condition and progress. She also visited his school-teacher. Information about the home, if a residential school or hostel, included the number of children, the number and quality of staff, dormitory conditions, facilities for recreation, contact with relatives, discipline, emotional atmosphere, and the general well-being of the children. About a foster-home the information would cover material conditions, the members of the household, and the attitude of the foster-parents to the child: note was taken of their competence as parents, their social interests and hobbies, their disciplinary rules, and their attitude to the child's relatives.

Information about the child would cover health, emotional well-being, social relations and hobbies, contact with relatives, general behaviour, and signs of nervousness or other abnormality. Notes about the informants and the apparent reliability of their reports were always included. About children in foster-homes, the foster-mother was the main informant, though the welfare officer provided invaluable supplementary information, enabling the foster-mother's account to be amplified and critically checked; similarly in children's homes and residential schools the warden or matron of the home was interviewed as well as the house-mother who had the child in her personal care; and further information was given by the children's officer about any changes of placement or other matters already disclosed.

The psychiatric social worker's interview with the school-teacher was designed to throw light on the child's educational attainments, his emotional and social adjustment in the school setting, and any abnormal conduct or nervous symptoms. The teacher was also asked whether the educational recommendations made at the Centre had been put into effect, and spontaneous comments about the foster-home, hostel, or other residence were noted.

88 Subsequent Histories: Outcome

(c) *Procedure: examination by psychiatrist.* I personally examined 96 of the 100 children, and I was often able at the same time to talk to the child's parent or foster-parent, or the matron or welfare officer. The interview followed much the same lines as when the child was examined on admission to Mersham, but special note was now taken of the child's attitude to his present home and the thoughts and wishes which he expressed about his parents. He was asked who he would go to for help if he were in trouble, and clues thus afforded were followed up; some children could only say 'I don't know: there isn't anyone', and one isolated child who had spent her life in institutions reiterated 'I would go to God'; she could not give the name of a single person in whom she could confide. When the child had named the person he most trusted, a similar inquiry was made and followed up about an adult of the sex opposite to that of the first-named adult whom he could look to for help; and questions were likewise asked about friendships with other children. These remarks threw light on the child's other statements about his parents and the people around him. His sleep and dreams were also inquired into. Information was obtained, especially from the smaller children, by indirect methods: the child was asked to draw a person and then to draw anything else he liked; the drawings provided a peg for significant emotional and other associations. Similarly a few children who were of low intelligence or less than 5 years old were observed while playing with a set of toys which represented a family.

It was feared that some of the children would be so unco-operative or ill at ease that rapport would be difficult. Fortunately this did not occur. The care with which the children's department arranged the visits—the child was told that he was to see the doctor who knew him at Mersham and who now wanted to hear how he was getting on—and the pleasant memories the children usually retained of their stay at the Centre, made them interested to see the psychiatrist again; indeed several asked if they could return to Mersham for a visit. Only four children could not be examined: a very psychopathic mother, whose daughter had been treated with striking benefit at a psychiatric hospital, nevertheless refused to let any doctor see her again; another mother, whose son, after a long delay, had been admitted to a school for maladjusted children and then

Subsequent Histories: Outcome 89

discharged as unsuitable, was too resentful to sanction an interview; a third mother whose husband had recently died was afraid that an interview with her son, who had been devoted to his father, would revive his grief; and a probation officer struggling with a very sensitive delinquent asked for the proposed interview to be cancelled.

3. ASSESSMENT OF FOLLOW-UP DATA

(*a*) *Method employed.* As the foregoing account of the lines of inquiry suggests, the condition of the child two years after his stay in the Reception Centre was assessed under several heads, but a general or summary estimate was called for, and this was made within five categories, defined as follows:

Very good: the child is contented with his home and surroundings, and in satisfactory contact with his father and mother or with their substitutes; he is socially well adjusted, making progress at school, and free from neurotic symptoms, delinquency, or other disorders of behaviour.

Good: the child is contented with his home and surroundings; if away from his own home, his relationship to his parents is not entirely satisfactory, but is adequately bolstered up by his affectionate relationship with the woman who is now his mother's substitute and often with the man who stands for his father; if he is at home with his parents (or with one parent) the relationship is satisfactory but the child's material needs are not fully provided for. He is making progress at school.

Fair: the child has a moderately satisfactory emotional relationship with parents or substitutes, but shows some defect in his educational progress or in his contentment with his surroundings; there are sometimes mild neurotic symptoms or mild delinquent behaviour.

Poor: the child has an unsatisfactory emotional relationship with parents or substitutes; he is unhappy and ill adjusted to his surroundings, and at times shows neurotic symptoms or delinquent behaviour.

Very poor: the child has an unsatisfactory relationship with parents, other adults, and often with children; he shows marked neurotic or other disorders of behaviour, and his personality is psychopathic.

In arriving at an assessment, a major difficulty was to assign the right significance to apparently transitory disturbances. If, for example, administrative difficulties in a children's home, changes of staff in a hostel, or decision by foster-parents to move house and no longer look after him have severed a child's emotional attachments or even suddenly rendered him homeless, it is no light matter shortly afterwards to classify that child's general state. The child's behaviour before the disturbing event, and his changing behaviour after it, were, of course, weighed; but there can be no finality in such a provisional assessment, nor, indeed, in any assessment made at a particular moment in the child's life when so much that is latent, so many stresses that have yet to be met, cannot be taken into account. But such interim judgements are not without value; they may even have implications for the future; but they must remain incomplete, relative, and revocable as a check.

A comparison was also made between the child's general condition as recorded initially at the Centre and that found two years later. The comparison was in part made by determining how far the child had moved in either direction in the ranking that ranged from 'very good' to 'very poor', and partly by assigning a numerical value to each of twenty-four characters relevant to progress so that a quantitative expression of improvement or deterioration was available.

(*b*) *Reliability of postal inquiries.* As remarked earlier the results of a home visit and interview with the 100 children in the special sample were expected to show whether replies to an inquiry by post could be regarded as trustworthy.

The postal replies did not permit a distinction to be made between 'good' and 'very good'. Nevertheless, the child's total condition could be fairly confidently classified in accordance with the criteria set out on page 89. In Table 49 it will be seen that for the majority (63) of the children comprised in the special sample of 100 the reports tallied (numbers italicized). There remained 37 about whom the reports disagreed. These called for closer scrutiny.

It was found that for 18 of the 37 children events had intervened between the postal inquiry and the special follow-up which seemed to account for the discrepancies. The personal visits and psychiatric interviews had perforce to be planned to

Subsequent Histories: Outcome

meet the convenience of several people and to take account of geographical or administrative needs; thus there could be an interval of months between the postal and the personal inquiries. The most common intercurrent event was the child's removal from one home or institution to another; next most common was the withdrawal of parental interest and loss of contact between the child and his parents or his actual desertion by them; and some of the children had left school and started work or had changed school. Of the 18 children just considered, 11 were in worse condition at the later personal inquiry than they had been at the time of the postal inquiry; 7 were in better condition.

TABLE 49

CONDITION OF CHILDREN TWO YEARS AFTER RECEPTION

(*Special inquiry and postal inquiry*)

	POSTAL INQUIRY				
Special inquiry	*Good*	*Fair*	*Poor*	*Very poor*	TOTAL
Very good and good	31	7	1	..	39
Fair . . .	12	19	4	1	36
Poor . . .	3	7	12	1	23
Very poor . .	..	..	1	1	2
TOTAL . .	46	33	18	3	100

In 5 more of the 37 subjects of discordant reports differences in the two assessments turned on additional or trifling points which could as easily have been interpreted favourably as unfavourably. For example, a child's condition had been called 'fair' because, according to the postal report, he was babyish and pilfered from his easy-going foster-mother but was otherwise satisfactory: in the special follow-up he was judged 'poor', evidently because there were fuller details and more emphasis on his pilfering and immature ways; there were other minor differences between the two reports but substantially they were similar.

The fourteen remaining discrepancies between the two assessments included one in which the postal report had been misleading; the informant had taken insufficient trouble and essential facts had not been communicated. The other thirteen postal reports had been too optimistic; they had taken too complacent a view. The discrepancies were not wide: no child whose condition was found by visit to be 'poor' had been classified by postal report as 'good' or 'very good' but only as 'fair'; nor had any found to be 'very poor' been postally classified as 'fair' or 'good'. However, the postal reports had given a rather more favourable picture than was found to be warranted. All these thirteen children were showing neurotic symptoms or depression which could be recognized in a medical interview but had been minimized or overlooked by those who responded to the postal inquiry, because the symptoms in question had not had an overtly disturbing effect on the child's conduct.

The main result of the comparison of the two types of report is to show an amount of agreement which, in view of the different character of the two inquiries, exceeded expectation. Nevertheless, the discrepancies, though understandable, make it unsafe to treat the replies to postal inquiries with the same confidence as the findings of special visits and interviews by skilled observers. Therefore, in what follows, the data relating outcome to possible causal factors will be set down separately for the selected 100 who were specially visited and for all other children (140) who had also been away from the Centre for at least two years. In some tables only the 100 specially visited children will be considered because only on them were the data sufficiently full and reliable.

The 140 children on whom only postal data were available included 72 who had been admitted to the Centre at an earlier date than the 100 personally visited children, and 68 who were admitted at a later date. The children in the postal inquiry were not consecutive admissions because information was lacking about some who had returned home or were in employment; hence the group largely comprises children living in foster-homes, children's homes, residential schools, approved schools, and boarding-schools. The period over which they were admitted to the Centre stretches from October 1947 to March 1948 (six months) and from December 1948 to August 1949 (nine months). (The personally visited children, it will be recalled, were admitted in the course of the eight months April–December 1948.)

Subsequent Histories: Outcome

4. OUTCOME OF RECOMMENDATIONS AND CONSEQUENT ACTION

(a) *General considerations*. The follow-up inquiry, as already remarked, was designed to answer two main questions: what effect for good or ill is traceable to the child's admission to Mersham and the consequent action taken; and what factors determine the short-term outcome.

Since there is no control group of similar children whose problems were not considered by a reception centre, it is clearly impossible to determine whether changes for better or worse in these children were due to what was done and recommended at the Reception Centre and to the action taken afterwards. Nevertheless, it is not unreasonable to suppose that conspicuous improvement or deterioration in the behaviour and well-being of the children may be attributed, at least in part, to the influence of the Reception Centre, and that a comparison between the subsequent histories of those children for whom the recommendations made at the Centre were carried out and those for whom they were not carried out could likewise bear on our problem.

TABLE 50

CONDITION OF CHILDREN AT RECEPTION AND TWO YEARS LATER

Condition of children	100 CHILDREN INCLUDED IN SPECIAL INQUIRY		140 CHILDREN INCLUDED IN POSTAL INQUIRY	
	At reception	Two years later	At reception	Two years later
Good	15	39	15 (11%)	64 (46%)
Fair	25	36	35 (25%)	45 (32%)
Poor	39	22	67 (48%)	23 (16%)
Very poor	21	3	23 (16%)	8 (6%)
TOTAL	100	100	140 (100%)	140 (100%)

The general trend of improvement is plain (Table 50). As a table of this kind does not disclose how many individual children improved and how many deteriorated, it is also necessary to compare the children's condition when they were personally visited two years after reception with the improvement or otherwise that had occurred during the two years (Table 51).

In this table, 'much improved' means that the child had, as it were, climbed three points in the scale, i.e. he had passed from 'very poor' to 'good'; similarly 'moderately improved' denotes passage from 'very poor' to 'fair', or from 'poor' to 'good'; 'slightly improved' means one move up only: of the eight children recorded as 'worse', none had moved down more than one place.

TABLE 51

CHANGE IN CONDITION OF CHILDREN TWO YEARS AFTER RECEPTION

(100 *children included in special inquiry*)

Change in condition of children since reception	CONDITION OF CHILDREN AT TIME OF SPECIAL INQUIRY				
	Good	*Fair*	*Poor*	*Very poor*	TOTAL
Much improved	7	..	..	..	7
Moderately improved	12	9	..	..	21
Slightly improved	12	16	7	..	35
No change	8	8	11	2	29
Worse . .	..	3	4	1	8
TOTAL	39	36	22	3	100

These findings indicate a considerable general improvement in well-being when compared with the condition on reception. It might be suspected that this recorded improvement was specious and reflects the bias of an assessor who exaggerates changes for the better and minimizes those for the worse. Since it was held that the advantages of a uniform assessment by one investigator who had examined all the children and used consistent standards outweighed the disadvantages of such a procedure, I assessed the condition of every child at the reception stage and the follow-up stage. The possibility of checking these assessments by obtaining independent estimates from other judges, using the same reports and descriptions, was considered, and some trials were made. But the conclusions reached by those who tried to classify the general psychological condition of a child they had not seen, purely on the strength of descriptive documents written by people they did not know, proved so unreliable that the effort was abandoned.

Subsequent Histories: Outcome

Table 52 shows that prominent symptoms of neurosis or disturbed behaviour were appreciably less prevalent among the

TABLE 52

CONDITION OF CHILDREN AT RECEPTION AND TWO YEARS LATER. NEUROTIC AND ANTI-SOCIAL FEATURES

(100 *children included in special inquiry*)

Neurotic and anti-social features		On reception	Two years later
Pilfering	Moderate	21	9
	Serious	7	1
Wandering, truancy	Moderate	14	6
	Serious	8	2
Destructive	Moderate	12	1
	Serious	0	0
Quarrelsome	Moderate	10	5
	Serious	1	0
Temper outbursts	Moderate	12	9
	Serious	2	0
Bullying	Moderate	12	7
	Serious	1	0
Sexual misdemeanours	Moderate	4	5
	Serious	4	1
Other anti-social	Moderate	20	14
	Serious	3	1
Anxiety	Moderate	22	41
	Serious	27	9
Timidity	Moderate	22	21
	Serious	6	3
Sleep disturbances	Moderate	12	10
	Serious	0	2
Eating disturbances	Moderate	3	2
	Serious	0	1
Excretory disturbances	Moderate	31	13
	Serious	6	2
Morbid fears	Moderate	9	15
	Serious	3	1
Tics, habits	Moderate	17	19
	Serious	4	3
Obsessional traits	Moderate	1	4
	Serious	1	0
Other neurotic	Moderate	13	14
	Serious	7	3

hundred visited children than they had been at the time of their reception; the improvement is least evident as far as manifestations of anxiety, including timidity, and morbid fears are concerned. The item 'other anti-social' includes lying and defiance of authority as well as excessive demands for attention; the item 'other neurotic' includes emotional immaturity, excessive daydreaming, ideas of reference, withdrawal, and stammering. The extent to which neurotic traits have persisted, whereas delinquent and cognate behaviour (which other people resent and fear) has lessened, confirms the view that it is easier to influence the outward signs and form of maladjustment in a child than to get him well adjusted and mentally healthy. Since the social aspects of the child's behaviour are usually uppermost in the minds of those who have him in their daily care or bear official responsibility for him, and since the repressive forces working to prevent objectionable behaviour are strong, it is understandable that the trends of response should be as the table indicates. But this does not mean that no essential improvement has been achieved, that only the form of the children's maladjustment has been changed, or that such environmental changes as were made had, or could have, little influence on neurotic and other disturbances in the children. There is clearly a great reduction in the frequency and severity of almost all the anomalies listed (though of course it falls short of what would be hoped for). The improvement is still more evident in the individual case-histories of the children. The environmental changes, which included changes in the children's human surroundings and upbringing, no doubt contributed to bring it about. Several children had been originally referred to Mersham from child-guidance clinics because expert treatment, given while the children remained at home, had failed to alter disturbing symptoms and behaviour. When the follow-up inquiry was made, these abnormalities were found to have disappeared.

(*b*) *Outcome related to placement.* The placement of the child was always the crucial and the most difficult decision. If recommendations had been drawn up as though for an ideal world in which wise and kindly foster-parents abounded, sensible psychiatrists were everywhere at hand to give treatment, parents always followed the course which was plainly in the child's best interests, and residential homes and institutions could be found of just the right size and type to suit each individual—if recommendations had been made in this spirit, they would perhaps have looked well on paper and would have

Subsequent Histories: Outcome 97

seemed—at any rate to those who put them forward—to provide far more favourable prospects for the child than the recommendations which were in fact made. But the practical circumstances were far from this ideal. Recommendations were therefore restricted to measures that were practicable or possible. Many administrative changes were taking place at that time following the passing of the Children Act 1948. There was a dearth of facilities, especially for maladjusted children. Foster-homes were few during the post-war period of acute housing shortage. Advice about placement had to take account of these conditions. Often it was impossible for the children's officer and other welfare workers to carry out our recommendation within a reasonable period of time—perhaps not for many months, during which the child had perforce to return to his own (unsatisfactory) home or to an institution: sometimes the recommendation could not be carried out at all. Expediency and compromise are therefore written large over the arrangements for placement: the wonder was, not that the recommendation had to be modified to second or third best, but that in so many cases satisfactory arrangements could be made at all. Those familiar with the procedure adopted in earlier years were in no doubt that the Mersham Centre and the children's department between them were now able to place deprived children more carefully and satisfactorily than had been possible before.

TABLE 53

CONDITION OF CHILDREN TWO YEARS AFTER RECEPTION RELATED TO PLACEMENT

(100 *children included in special inquiry*)

Placement	CONDITION OF CHILDREN TWO YEARS AFTER RECEPTION			TOTAL
	Good	Fair	Poor	
Placed as recommended . . .	31	29	15	75
Not placed as recommended . .	8	7	10	25

It is evident (Table 53) that children placed as recommended are a rather more satisfactory group two years later than those in respect of whom the recommendations had not been put into effect. Of the 75 children placed as recommended, 80 per cent.

were in good or fair condition; but of the 25 not so placed, only 60 per cent.

If the change in the children's condition rather than their absolute state at the end of the period is set against the action taken, the same conclusion can be drawn (Table 54). Bearing in mind that several of the twenty-nine children who showed no change had been classed as 'good' on their reception, the reader will see that the proportion who definitely improved (24, i.e. 32 per cent.) among those placed as recommended compares favourably with the proportion definitely improved (4, i.e. 16 per cent.) among those not placed as recommended.

TABLE 54
CHANGE IN CONDITION OF CHILDREN TWO YEARS AFTER RECEPTION RELATED TO PLACEMENT
(100 *children included in special inquiry*)

Placement	Much improved	Moderately improved	Slightly improved	No change	Worse	TOTAL
Placed as recommended	6	18	24	22	5	75
Not placed as recommended	1	3	11	7	3	25

Much restraint is necessary in evaluating such findings, for there are complicating factors which enjoin caution: delays in securing a suitable place for the child; changes from one home to another (because he has not settled or for extraneous reasons); insistent demands by parents for his return; and the obstacles in finding a suitable home for an unresponsive or delinquent child. Some of these factors may have lessened the apparent value of the placement recommended and carried out, and others may have enhanced it.

Table 55 shows that outcome, judged by the proportions of children whose condition is assessed as good or fair, differs with placement. Taking the figures of both inquiries together, 44 out of 55 children placed in foster-homes did well compared with 6 out of 13 placed in approved schools. Obviously, however, the problems and condition of the children sent to one kind of place, e.g. approved schools, may differ from those of children sent to another, e.g. foster-homes. We should not suppose, therefore,

Subsequent Histories: Outcome 99

that a particular sort of place is necessarily preferable to another because more of the children sent there were doing well. To obtain a full picture, the condition of the children at the time of reception and the subsequent changes must be taken into account.

TABLE 55

CONDITION OF CHILDREN TWO YEARS AFTER RECEPTION RELATED TO TYPE OF PLACEMENT

Placement	CONDITION OF CHILDREN TWO YEARS AFTER RECEPTION							
	100 included in special inquiry				*140 included in postal inquiry*			
	Good	Fair	Poor	TOTAL	Good	Fair	Poor	TOTAL
Returned to parents	5	7	4	16	6	3	7	16
Foster-home	13	10	5	28	15	6	6	27
Boarding-school	2	2	2	6	8	7	1	16
Children's home or nursery	8	9	5	22	30	14	6	50
Adjustment hostel	5	3	3	11	..	5	1	6
School for maladjusted	1	..	1	2	1	5	7	13
School for educationally subnormal pupils	2	3	..	5	..	1	1	2
Approved school	2	..	4	6	1	3	3	7
Other	1	2	1	4	1	2	..	3
TOTAL	39	36	25	100	62	46	32	140

Of 240 children shown in Table 56, 151 (63 per cent.) were assessed as having changed for the better and 14 (6 per cent.) as having changed for the worse two years after admission. In reality the improvement may have been somewhat less pronounced than the figures convey because this table is based on the combined results of the two follow-up inquiries, one of which (the postal inquiry) gave too favourable a picture. Nevertheless, it is fairly clear that no type of placement had a monopoly of successes, that none had a generally adverse effect, and that none was chosen for an undue proportion of the thirty well-adjusted children whose condition was rated as 'good' on admission, though some types of placements (the last five) were chosen almost entirely for children who had been in poor condition at the outset.

Study of individual case-records underlines the commonsense view that the outcome depends less on whether the child

Subsequent Histories: Outcome

TABLE 56

CHANGE IN CONDITION OF CHILDREN TWO YEARS AFTER RECEPTION RELATED TO TYPE OF PLACEMENT

(*Special inquiry and postal inquiry*)

Placement	CONDITION AT TIME OF RECEPTION				CHANGE DURING ENSUING TWO YEARS		
	Good	*Fair*	*Poor*	TOTAL	*Improved*	*Same*	*Worse*
Returned to parents .	5	13	14	32	11	17	4
Foster-home . .	12	17	26	55	27	25	3
Boarding-school .	5	6	11	22	13	8	1
Children's home or nursery . .	5	22	45	72	56	11	5
Adjustment hostel .	1	..	16	17	14	3	..
School for maladjusted	..	..	15	15	10	4	1
School for educationally subnormal pupils	1	..	6	7	5	2	..
Approved school .	..	1	12	13	9	4	..
Other . . .	1	..	6	7	6	1	..
TOTAL . . .	30	59	151	240	151	75	14

is placed in, say, a boarding-school or a foster-home, than on the internal conditions of his new home, the size and personality of the staff, the contacts maintained with relatives, and the opportunities and outlets afforded to the child. There seems to be no inherent virtue in a foster-home that makes it always preferable to an institution; but a good foster-home is certainly better than an indifferent institution, and an average foster-home probably better than an average institution. On the other hand, the bad foster-home, where the child does not receive affection and understanding, is probably worse than the small institution where these essential needs are satisfied, especially if he has the chance, for some weeks or months every year, of returning to the home of friends or relatives, as does the boarding-school child during the holidays.

(*c*) *Outcome related to other recommended measures.* Besides advice on placement, recommendations were made under one or more of the following eight headings:

(i) Keeping the child in physical and psychological touch with his brothers and sisters by arranging for them to be sent to the same place or to a place near by.

(ii) Keeping him in touch with his parents provided that they

Subsequent Histories: Outcome

were not cruel, unloving, or hostile to him. Such contact was desirable even when parents had been sent to prison for neglecting their children. A man, for instance, who had quarrelled incessantly with his wife and had been indifferent to his children, was encouraged to visit them with her after leaving jail; thereafter the family became more united. Parents handicapped by mental disabilities and misfortune, if relieved of excessive burdens, can helpfully resume some responsibility for their children. Sometimes, by taking the children back into their homes, parents were even brought to the point of resuming full responsibilities. But in cases of gross parental neglect such a complete rehabilitation was rare.

(iii) Arranging for children to spend short holidays with relatives or, if suitable relatives were not available, with an interested family whom they might visit frequently ('aunt' and 'uncle' schemes).

(iv) Adoption for some friendless young children.

(v) Psychiatric treatment.

(vi) Educational management.

(vii) Vocational placement.

(viii) Physical health.

Recommendations were sometimes carried out in full, but this was not always possible, as for example when the education authority could not provide individual coaching for very backward children.

TABLE 57

CONDITION OF CHILDREN TWO YEARS AFTER RECEPTION RELATED TO ACTION TAKEN ON RECOMMENDATIONS (OTHER THAN PLACEMENT)

(95 *children included in special inquiry**)

Recommendations other than placement	CONDITION TWO YEARS AFTER RECEPTION			TOTAL
	Good	Fair	Poor	
Carried out	15	12	9	36
Partly carried out	21	14	4	39
Not carried out	2	8	10	20
TOTAL	38	34	23	95

* Recommendations for the remaining five of these children had been exclusively concerned with placement.

Table 57 suggests that total failure to carry out the recommendations made the prospect bleaker for the child, or alternatively that such failure occurred chiefly in the most intractable and unpromising children. The findings do not justify separate consideration of each of the eight recommendations listed above with the exception of those relating to the child's contact with his parents or other close adult relatives.

TABLE 58

CHILDREN'S CONDITION TWO YEARS AFTER RECEPTION RELATED TO NATURE OF CONTACT WITH PARENTS OR CLOSE RELATIVES

Condition two years after reception	CONTACT WITH PARENTS OR RELATIVES						
	100 children included in special inquiry			140 children included in postal inquiry			
	Living at home	Satisfactory, regular	Un-satisfactory	Living at home	Satisfactory, regular	Un-satisfactory	Unknown
Good . .	7	22	10	11	32	10	9
Fair . .	6	14	16	8	23	13	2
Poor . .	3	11	11	11	7	9	5
TOTAL .	16	47	37	30	62	32	16

Children who have satisfactory contacts with their parents or other adults among their close relatives do better than those who have few or no contacts of this kind (Table 58). Out of 155 children, 72 (47 per cent.) who were living at home or having satisfactory contact with parents or adult relatives were in good condition, but only 20 out of 69 children (29 per cent.) whose contacts were unsatisfactory. Cause and effect, however, are difficult to distinguish. The relationship is no doubt reciprocal: children in good touch with close relatives gain thereby, and parents are more likely to keep in touch with responsive children.

The character of a child's contact with parents or relatives can scarcely be shown in a table. In the figures given, contact has been considered satisfactory if the child visited or spent holidays with parents or relatives and received from them frequent letters and parcels, or if parents living near by visited the child at least once a month.

5. OUTCOME RELATED TO OTHER CIRCUMSTANCES AT TIME OF RECEPTION

(a) *Outcome related to attitude of parents.* A child's development depends much on the affection and care he has received from

Subsequent Histories: Outcome

his parents; the strength and warmth of early family ties continue to exert an influence even after a child has left home. A child who has been cruelly treated and rejected might be expected to do well away from home; but continued exposure from early childhood to the dislike or indifference of parents may have so warped his nature that kindliness and affection at a later stage may fail to evoke a good response. An unequivocal connexion between the parents' affection, or lack of it, and the condition of the child two years after he was first seen at the Centre cannot be expected; but some connexion is suggested by Table 59. It shows that, of 138 children (54 plus 84) with affectionate mothers, 118 or 85 per cent. were in good or fair condition; whereas, of 71 children whose mothers were assessed as 'not normally affectionate', only 43 or 61 per cent. were in good or fair condition. Some of the mothers listed as 'not normally affectionate' were over-indulgent mothers.

TABLE 59
CHILDREN'S CONDITION TWO YEARS AFTER RECEPTION RELATED TO MOTHER'S AFFECTION AT TIME OF RECEPTION

Condition two years after reception	100 CHILDREN INCLUDED IN SPECIAL INQUIRY			140 CHILDREN INCLUDED IN POSTAL INQUIRY		
	Mother dead or deserted child	Mother normally affectionate	Mother not normally affectionate	Mother dead or deserted child	Mother normally affectionate	Mother not normally affectionate
Good	5	24	10	6	38	20
Fair	5	20	11	7	36	2
Poor	2	10	13	6	10	15
TOTAL	12	54	34	19	84	37

It almost appears as if maternal neglect is favourable for a child's progress (Table 60). This paradox is at least partly explained by the fact that children admitted to the Centre on account of neglect were often emotionally stable, whereas those admitted for other reasons usually had troubles of behaviour and personality which augured ill for their progress. Of 71 (29 plus 42) children whose mothers were attentive to their needs, 49 (70 per cent.) were in good or fair condition, as against 112 (81 per cent.) of the 138 children with neglectful mothers.

TABLE 60
CHILDREN'S CONDITION TWO YEARS AFTER RECEPTION RELATED TO MOTHER'S SOLICITUDE AT TIME OF RECEPTION

	100 CHILDREN INCLUDED IN SPECIAL INQUIRY			140 CHILDREN INCLUDED IN POSTAL INQUIRY		
Condition two years after reception	Mother dead or deserted child	Mother attentive to child's needs	Mother neglectful	Mother dead or deserted child	Mother attentive to child's needs	Mother neglectful
Good	5	8	26	6	18	40
Fair	5	11	20	7	12	26
Poor	2	10	13	6	12	13
TOTAL	12	29	59	19	42	79

TABLE 61
CHILDREN'S CONDITION TWO YEARS AFTER RECEPTION RELATED TO FATHER'S AFFECTION AT TIME OF RECEPTION

	100 CHILDREN INCLUDED IN SPECIAL INQUIRY			140 CHILDREN INCLUDED IN POSTAL INQUIRY		
Condition two years after reception	Father dead or deserted child	Normally affectionate	Not normally affectionate	Father dead or deserted child	Normally affectionate	Not normally affectionate
Good	7	17	15	22	9	33
Fair	6	15	15	5	18	22
Poor	6	8	11	10	6	15
TOTAL	19	40	41	37	33	70

TABLE 62
CHILDREN'S CONDITION TWO YEARS AFTER RECEPTION RELATED TO FATHER'S SOLICITUDE AT TIME OF RECEPTION

	100 CHILDREN INCLUDED IN SPECIAL INQUIRY			140 CHILDREN INCLUDED IN POSTAL INQUIRY		
Condition two years after reception	Father dead or deserted child	Father attentive to child's needs	Father neglectful	Father dead or deserted child	Father attentive to child's needs	Father neglectful
Good	7	14	18	22	23	19
Fair	6	13	17	5	25	15
Poor	6	9	10	10	7	14
TOTAL	19	36	45	37	55	48

Subsequent Histories: Outcome

No significant relation can be found between the children's condition and the attitudes of their fathers (Tables 61 and 62).

(b) *Outcome related to previous separation from parents.* Common sense suggests that a child who is separated from his mother at an early age suffers from this deprivation and may, in some cases, suffer irremediable harm. Much evidence has been collected to confirm this view, but we have already explained in the previous chapter that it would be wrong at this stage of our knowledge to attribute certain characteristics of personality to the effects of maternal deprivation, as some people have done, or to expect that all children separated from their mothers will show ill effects. Children brought up in institutions—and, of course, children in foster-homes—are not necessarily cut off from warm affection by a mother-substitute; they are certainly more likely to receive it than the children studied by Goldfarb, who were living in a highly impersonal environment.

If the contentions of Bender, Lowrey, Goldfarb, Bowlby, and Spitz were correct, many of the Mersham children who had been separated from their mothers at an early age should not only exhibit an affectionless, psychopathic character, but should be relatively fixed in this mould, their behaviour being unlikely to improve. Many of them either did not have 'any opportunity for forming an attachment to a mother-figure during the first three years', or had suffered 'deprivation for a limited period—at least three months and probably more than six—during the first three or four years', or had had 'changes from one mother-figure to another during the same period'.[1] It is also asserted that, although the effects of early damage through deprivation can be greatly reduced by good mothering, 'Goldfarb's work demonstrates without any doubt . . . that such mothering is almost useless if delayed until the age of $2\frac{1}{2}$ years. . . . In actual fact this upper age-limit for most babies is probably before twelve months.'

The findings in Table 63 suggest that the children who had been separated from their mothers at some age before reception were rather less satisfactory two years after reception than the rest. But the difference is not substantial. Moreover, of all the children 'permanently' separated from their mothers before the age of 5 about a third are in satisfactory condition, and another

[1] J. Bowlby, *Maternal Care and Mental Health*, W.H.O., Geneva, 1951, p. 47.

106   *Subsequent Histories: Outcome*

TABLE 63

CHILDREN'S CONDITION TWO YEARS AFTER RECEPTION RELATED TO SEPARATION FROM MOTHER FOR MORE THAN 3 MONTHS BEFORE RECEPTION

Separation from mother before reception	100 children included in special inquiry				140 children included in postal inquiry				240 children (both inquiries)			
	Good	Fair	Poor	TOTAL	Good	Fair	Poor	TOTAL	Good	Fair	Poor	TOTAL
Not separated	22	14	5	41	25	13	12	50	47	27	17	91
Separated more than 3 months	17	22	20	59	39	32	19	90	56	54	39	149
TOTAL	39	36	25	100	64	45	31	140	103	81	56	240
Separated before age of 2 years	3	3	4	10	13	8	1	22	16	11	5	32
Separated between ages of 2 and 5 years	9	10	7	26	14	9	8	31	23	19	15	57
Separated after age of 5 years	5	9	9	23	12	15	10	37	17	24	19	60

third are fairly satisfactory. The cases of most serious harm should be found among those children who had been separated from their mothers for long periods or permanently before the age of 2 years, but Table 64 does not indicate that by the criteria here employed they were in a conspicuously worse condition than the other children in the sample of 240.

Case-records of a few such children illustrate how varying their progress may be over a period of two or three years. The following are summary records of three children (Nellie, Richard, and William) whose condition was considered 'good'. They were all separated from their mothers before the age of 2.

Nellie, born 24.12.37, was an illegitimate child, reared in one nursery home until she was 10 months old, then in another until her maternal grandmother (who had visited her and paid for her) died. The child was then adopted (in October 1942) by a couple who had one child of their own. The adoptive mother was herself an illegitimate child who had been adopted by unkind people; she was chronically depressed, with exacerbations which on two occasions (September 1946 and September 1947) were treated without much benefit by E.C.T.[1] at a psychiatric centre. Nellie, who had been considered pleasant and affectionate at the nursery home, was rather wilful and educationally backward after adoption, but until her adoptive mother's mental disturbance she was well adjusted. She then began rocking and making a noise at night, and was tomboyish in the daytime. She was very attached to her home and, when sent to stay with friends in 1947, she ran away, walking the 15 miles home.

TABLE 64

CHILDREN'S CONDITION TWO YEARS AFTER RECEPTION RELATED TO SEPARATION FROM THEIR MOTHERS AT DIFFERENT AGES BEFORE RECEPTION

(*Numbers only*)

	CHILDREN'S CONDITION TWO YEARS AFTER RECEPTION (S) = Special inquiry. (P) = Postal inquiry.											
Separation from mother before reception	Good			Fair			Poor			TOTAL		
	S.	P.	TOTAL	S.	P.	TOTAL	S.	P.	TOTAL	S.	P.	TOTAL
Not separated	22	25	47	14	13	27	5	12	17	41	50	91
Temporary separation *before* age of 2 years	2	3	5	..	5	5	2	..	2	4	8	12
Temporary separation *after* age of 2 years	5	19	24	13	9	22	8	9	17	26	37	63
Lasting separation *before* age of 2 years	1	10	11	3	3	6	2	1	3	6	14	20
Lasting separation between ages of 2 to 5 years	4	2	6	5	8	13	5	6	11	14	16	30
Lasting separation after age of 5 years	5	5	10	1	7	8	3	3	6	9	15	24
TOTAL	39	64	103	36	45	81	25	31	56	100	140	240
All separated more than 3 months	17	39	56	22	32	54	20	19	39	59	90	149

When admitted to Mersham in May 1948, she was very upset at having to leave her adoptive father and continued to be unsettled, sometimes crying, at other times skipping and playing like a tomboy. She ate erratically. During the second week of her stay and thereafter she became more composed, took her meals, played games with the other children and responded pleasantly to adults, though still tense and fidgety. She had impaired vision in the right eye, right internal strabismus, and nystagmus. From Mersham she went to a small hostel with a mild religious atmosphere, housing twelve maladjusted girls, where she has remained. She attended a nearby child-guidance clinic: her adoptive parents concurred in this arrangement because of the mother's mental condition.

The child settled at the hostel and she was not upset by visits from

[1] Electric convulsion therapy.

her adoptive parents. In April 1950 the question of her return home was discussed with her parents and it was agreed to be inadvisable, as she was doing well and her adoptive mother could not be relied on to give her 'good steady handling'. But she went home during the long school holidays. Rocking had ceased but began again for a short while after her return from home. By March 1951, when I interviewed her, she had developed physically, had begun to menstruate, and was outwardly well adjusted. She slept well and had no neurotic fears or other symptoms except that she blinked and was fidgety and embarrassed with strangers. She was active at games, a keen Girl Guide, and popular, with a good sense of humour. There was no evidence of delinquency or lack of affection.

Richard aged 6 years and 4 months was admitted in January 1949 because of temper outbursts and destructiveness in his foster-home, disobedience and aggressive behaviour at school, and sexual curiosity. He had also suffered from frequent attacks of asthma which had prevented him from going to school regularly and from making outside social contacts. He was an illegitimate child handed over to the care of the local authority at 8 months; he had been in five different nurseries before he was placed at 2 years 10 months with his foster-parents. They were experienced and kindly but elderly and without the necessary energy to interest and discipline so young and active a child.

At the Reception Centre he was found to be of average intelligence. He had a lively curiosity and enjoyed group activities. He was observant but over-talkative and distractable. He showed no antisocial or aggressive behaviour. Occasionally he wet himself at night and by day; in a psychiatric interview he expressed some hostility towards his foster-mother, and said that the other children were trying to annoy him. He was somewhat preoccupied with his health and seemed afraid of getting ill. He had slight bronchial catarrh but was above average weight and in good condition apart from a cold. Undue attention had been paid to his physical care, and his illnesses had hindered the development of social and intellectual interests.

It was advised that he should have a short period (not more than three months) of treatment in an adjustment hostel before returning to his foster-parents and that they should be advised how to deal more sensibly with his curiosity (sexual and other), provide him with better outlets, and handle his asthmatic attacks with less outward concern. His school-teacher's aid was to be sought to help him with work missed through illness. His placement was to be reviewed again after three months. All these measures were carried out

Subsequent Histories: Outcome 109

(except that he returned home without a vacancy having been found for him in an adjustment hostel). He improved, became much happier, and developed a warm friendship for a neighbouring child. Unfortunately a year later his foster-father developed a fatal illness and needed his foster-mother's full-time care: Richard had to be sent to a new foster-home. But he was not happy there, and his new foster-mother asked for his removal after seven months. As it was considered unwise to risk another failure in a foster-home, he was placed in a boys' home in the country which could take 20–30 children. Contact with his first foster-mother was kept up by visits and letters. He formed a strong attachment to the superintendent of the home, was moderately affectionate towards his housemother, and got on well with other boys. He had a close friend of his own age but he was not fond of group activities. No neurotic symptoms and no delinquency were observed.

William, aged 9 years and 3 months, was admitted to the Centre because his foster-parents asked for advice. They complained that he had twice recently stolen a trifling sum of money from his foster-mother's purse and was unusually interested in playing with fire.

William had had no contact with his mother, who had puerperal mania at his birth; his father had died a year later. After birth he had been privately placed with foster-parents who neglected him. He was removed from their care at 18 months of age and placed in his present home. The foster-parents, who took him reluctantly, were a united couple, the father a competent craftsman particularly interested in the boy, the mother an over-anxious woman, prone to set very high standards for herself and others, and easily upset if anyone fell short. They had a much older son of their own and a foster-daughter who was three years William's senior; both these children were more competent and placid than William. After his arrival he responded rapidly to training, but he worried his foster-mother because he liked to play with matches and light fires. When he was $3\frac{1}{2}$ his foster-mother brought him to a child-guidance clinic because he had screaming attacks and was jealous of his foster-siblings. She did not attend again until shortly before William's admission to the Centre when he was 9. He had been found lighting a fire, and after being reprimanded had stolen a little money from her purse. At school he was reported to be making good progress and there were no complaints of his behaviour.

At the Reception Centre he seemed over-sensitive and over-controlled for a boy of his age; he was easily frightened by other children and discouraged to the verge of tears when asked to do something at which he thought he might fail. On intelligence tests his score was average; he was very critical of his mistakes and sometimes avoided making a decision. In a psychiatric interview his disturbance appeared to centre around a fear of standing badly with his foster-mother and of being sent away from her. He felt envious of the other two children in the home and thought they 'picked on' him. The foster-parents were interviewed, and it was evident that conditions in the home were largely responsible for the degree of anxiety and discouragement the boy now showed. The mother was over-anxious and rather regretted having accepted him as a foster-child; the foster-father was warmly disposed towards him and unaware of his wife's attitude. They were reassured that the boy's interests in lighting fires did not indicate a criminal tendency and could be turned into healthier channels. They were also told that he had not the serious mental abnormality which they had suspected in view of his mother's history. He improved very much, but some months later his foster-mother, who had become more anxious and tense, complained of his outbursts of temper. She and the child received psychiatric treatment for a short time. Two years after leaving Mersham William is still at this foster-home and is reported to be a friendly, happy boy, an enthusiastic Wolf Cub, well behaved, and working well in school.

It is obviously impracticable to reproduce here all the case-histories of children who were separated from their mothers in early life, but the instances given and those in Appendix 2 (Iris, Violet, Edward, and Kenneth), are fairly representative. They corroborate the findings set out in the tables. Neither statistical nor clinical study confirms the close, if not specific, connexion alleged between a child's early separation from his mother and the development of an affectionless or psychopathic character, so far as this can be observed during childhood and adolescence. Nor do the findings confirm the contention that the ill effects of separation are almost always beyond remedy by changes in environment and other therapeutic measures adapted to the needs of the individual child.

The undeniable ill effects on a child of being motherless and unloved may take many forms and may even possibly persist beneath a smooth surface to become manifest in adult life. But so far as the observable behaviour of children is concerned, the evidence in the present study does not suggest that this misfortune can be isolated as the prime cause of their troubles, without regard to the kind of mother the child has lost and the kind of care she gave him. It has been striking to observe in this

Subsequent Histories: Outcome

study that some children long exposed to the dislike or indifference of their natural mothers—and perhaps also of their fathers—gained rather than lost by separation, provided that they passed into kind and sensible hands. The results of separation depend on several factors: among them are the quality of the tie between mother (or mother and father) and child; the manner in which the child is prepared for the break; and the person or persons who must step into the parents' place. If these problems are correctly assessed and appropriately solved, separation from a callous or 'affectionless' parent may be a positive benefit to the child. So, at least, our findings would suggest. That is not to say that every child whose parents are indifferent should be separated from them or would be unharmed by such a separation. Clearly, efforts to change the parents' attitude, and to support them in their difficulties—which are so often the outcome of their own psychological disabilities—are called for to the fullest. Success in such efforts may leave the child better adjusted than if he had been removed from his family. If separation is unavoidable, it cannot be taken as proved—our findings suggest—that the younger the child, the graver the consequences. A child of 2 to 5 who cannot express, save by disturbed behaviour, his sense of loss and fear as he parts from all that has been *familiar*—an apt word, here reverting to its earlier meaning—such a child may be more gravely hurt by being taken to new and strange surroundings than an infant in his first year who is carefully piloted through the transition. Neither can it be taken as proved, in spite of assertions and some evidence, that an unsatisfactory parent is always to be preferred to an 'institution'. The word 'institution' unfortunately carries a taint and evokes a prejudice rooted in the history of our Poor Law, but if it be taken to include the many small hostels, nursery homes, and residential homes to which deprived children are sent, these have no common demerit but are good or bad according to the qualities of those who work in them and the rules they make. A child may develop more healthily in a good institution than in an indifferent or hostile family; but the effects of a bad institution are deplorable.

A child's separation from his father is likewise inimical to mental and social growth, but so many Mersham children had been separated from their fathers during the war that the number unseparated is too small for analysis. Nor could an adequate control group outside Mersham be found.

(c) *Outcome related to child's attitude to parents.* The warmth and spontaneity of a child's feeling, especially for his parents and for other children, would usually be taken as a favourable prognostic sign; the more capable of showing affection, the more likely is the child to evoke it in response, to thrive and to adapt himself to change. Many exceptions to this generalization spring to mind, but it is nevertheless worth while to test whether the outcome has been on the whole better in those children whose affections were warm.

The tendency is in the expected direction: the affectionate and sociable children did better in the two years after leaving Mersham than those who were cold or variable (Table 65) But too much could be read into a finding which is based on necessarily incomplete judgements; a child does not wear his heart on his sleeve, and his feelings may not be truly disclosed by his behaviour nor by his response when examined by a psychiatrist in a short interview. Some of the children had been long separated from their true mothers or fathers and it was their attitude to the best substitute for the missing parent that

TABLE 65

CHILDREN'S CONDITION TWO YEARS AFTER RECEPTION RELATED TO ATTITUDE AT RECEPTION TOWARDS PARENTS, PARENT-SUBSTITUTES, AND OTHER CHILDREN*

Child's attitude at time of reception	CHILDREN'S CONDITION TWO YEARS AFTER RECEPTION							
	100 children included in special inquiry				140 children included in postal inquiry			
	Good	Fair	Poor	TOTAL	Good	Fair	Poor	TOTAL
Affectionate to mother	33 (45)	26 (36)	14 (19)	73 (100)	46 (57·5)	20 (25)	14 (17·5)	80 (100)
Variable, cold or hostile to mother	6 (22)	10 (37)	11 (41)	27 (100)	18 (30)	25 (42)	17 (28)	60 (100)
Affectionate to father	24 (46)	20 (39)	8 (15)	52 (100)	36 (54)	24 (36)	7 (10)	67 (100)
Variable, cold or hostile to father	14 (32)	14 (32)	16 (36)	44 (100)	20 (33)	21 (34)	20 (33)	61 (100)
Attitude unknown	..	..	..	4	..	..	..	12
Socialbe with children	31 (45)	25 (36)	13 (19)	69 (100)	54 (55)	29 (30)	15 (15)	98 (100)
Rather unsociable or solitary	8 (26)	11 (35)	12 (39)	31 (100)	10 (24)	16 (38)	16 (38)	42 (100)

* Percentages in brackets.

Subsequent Histories: Outcome

was here recorded though in some cases there was no one who took the father's place.

The effect of arrangements made for the children at the Centre and afterwards could be partly gauged by comparing their attitudes when they first came to Mersham with their attitudes two years later. Only the personally visited children could supply the requisite data. Special attention was paid to this matter in the follow-up interviews both with the children and with the adults responsible for them.

TABLE 66

CHILDREN'S ATTITUDE TO MOTHER OR MOTHER-SUBSTITUTE AT RECEPTION AND TWO YEARS LATER

(100 *children included in special inquiry*)

Attitude to mother at time of reception	ATTITUDE TO MOTHER OR MOTHER-SUBSTITUTE TWO YEARS AFTER RECEPTION				
	Affectionate	*Rather cold*	*Very cold or hostile*	*Unknown*	TOTAL
Affectionate	59	9	5	..	73
Variable or rather cold	9	10	..	1	20
Very cold or hostile	5	1	1	..	7
TOTAL	73	20	6	1	100

Table 66 shows that the majority of the children did not deteriorate in this respect and some improved; a small number (five in each case) passed from one extreme to the other. When the change was for the worse, there had been no one to whom the child could give his affection: his mother had lost touch with him and no substitute had offered.

(d) *Outcome related to child's age.* The age at which a child was admitted to Mersham—often a turning-point in his life—would presumably be an important factor influencing his subsequent adjustment. But it is equally likely that the rather different reasons for referring children of different age-groups to the Centre, and the rather different placement arranged for them, would also affect the apparent association between age and outcome. It is evident from Table 67 that the 27 children who were under the age of 5 years when they came to the Reception Centre came off best during the ensuing two years: the condition of 17 was recorded as good, and of 10 as fair or poor.

114 *Subsequent Histories: Outcome*

The majority of these children under 5 were referred because they had been grossly neglected by their parents or had been orphaned through the death or desertion of both parents. They were mostly free from untoward behaviour or symptoms when received, and an effort was usually made to place them in a family, if possible with well-proved foster-parents. Four were sent back to their own parents, and five went to a children's home in an entire family group of brothers and sisters.

TABLE 67

CHILDREN'S CONDITION TWO YEARS AFTER RECEPTION RELATED TO AGE ON RECEPTION

Children's condition two years after reception	AGE ON RECEPTION									
	100 children included in special inquiry				140 children included in postal inquiry				240 children (both inquiries)		
	Under 5 years	5–7 years	8–11 years	12 years or over	Under 5 years	5–7 years	8–11 years	12 years or over	Under 5 years	5–7 years	8–11 years	12 years or over
Good	6	7	19	7	11	15	21	17	17	22	40	24
Fair	4	6	20	6	3	4	28	10	7	10	48	16
Poor	1	6	11	7	2	8	16	5	3	14	27	12
TOTAL	11	19	50	20	16	27	65	32	27	46	115	52

(e) *Outcome related to intelligence*. Table 68 shows that the proportion of children who do well among those of average or above-average intelligence is higher than the corresponding proportion among children with less than average intelligence. Placement, however, was influenced by intelligence: very dull children, for example, were seldom sent to foster-homes.

TABLE 68

CHILDREN'S CONDITION TWO YEARS AFTER RECEPTION RELATED TO INTELLIGENCE QUOTIENT AT TIME OF RECEPTION

Children's condition 2 years after reception	INTELLIGENCE QUOTIENT												
	100 children included in special inquiry					140 children included in postal inquiry					240 children (both inquiries)		
	Below 70	70–89	90–109	110–129	130 and above	Below 70	70–89	90–109	110–129	130 and above	Not tested	Under 90	Over 90	Not tested
Good	2	8	16	11	2	1	12	31	11	6	3	23	77	3
Fair	4	11	14	5	2	1	14	16	12	2	..	30	51	..
Poor	1	10	11	2	1	..	10	14	4	..	3	21	32	3
TOTAL	7	29	41	18	5	2	36	61	27	8	6	74	160	6

Subsequent Histories: Outcome 115

(*f*) *Outcome related to progress at school.* Since backwardness was a conspicuous feature of many of the Mersham children, a comparison was made, in respect of the 100 personally visited children, between their teachers' opinions of their school work at the time of reception and opinions of other teachers two years later. If fifteen children who had been below school age at the time of reception are omitted, the numbers of children then graded as 'good', 'fair', or 'poor' were 14, 16, and 55 respectively: two years later the corresponding figures were 19, 34, and 31. It would have been desirable to check this teachers' estimate by comparing the results of educational attainment tests, but this was not possible because such tests could not be given at the end of the follow-up period. But a comparison of the children's grading, from test-scores, at the time of reception with the rating given by their teachers two years later showed that only a few children had moved from the 'poor' to the 'fair' or 'good' class in arithmetic, and practically none in reading. So backward were many of these children educationally on admission (see Table 14, p. 35) and so backward do their teachers consider them still, that it seems a major problem to find a way of furthering their education and that of similarly handicapped children to the extent their innate intelligence permits. To place them in classes for backward children in ordinary schools, as was done in many of these cases, is not sufficient (though of course it makes life easier and perhaps happier for the time being). When judged by group tests of intelligence, many of these children may be thought mentally defective or dull; but it is well known that such tests are a deceptive index for emotionally disturbed children. The main scholastic need was for individual teaching, which cannot be supplied for all backward children within the educational system. Some of them could best obtain what they require from the educational psychiatrist of a child-guidance clinic; but here, too, practical difficulties—travelling, waiting-lists, and so forth—often intervene.

(*g*) *Outcome related to patterns of behaviour.* We can scarcely expect to find any hard-and-fast connexion between a pattern of behaviour exhibited at some point in a child's life and his general psychological and social well-being during the next two or three years. Confident predictions are too often falsified. It

Subsequent Histories: Outcome

might, however, be thought that one form of delinquency would be more persistent and more undesirable in its results than another, or that neurotic children might fare better, at any rate in the short run, than delinquent children.

TABLE 69

CHILDREN'S CONDITION TWO YEARS AFTER RECEPTION RELATED TO PATTERN OF BEHAVIOUR AT THE TIME OF RECEPTION

Behaviour pattern at time of reception	CONDITION TWO YEARS AFTER RECEPTION							
	100 children included in special inquiry			*140 children included in postal inquiry*			*240 children (both inquiries)*		
	Good	Fair	Poor	Good	Fair	Poor	Good	Fair	Poor
Normal	16	8	1	28	5	1	44	13	2
Unsocialized aggressive	1	1	1	7	7	8	8	8	9
Socialized delinquent	5	4	10	6	10	5	11	14	15
Inhibited, neurotic	4	7	8	6	6	5	10	13	13
Slightly delinquent	4	2	..	8	4	3	12	6	3
Slightly neurotic	8	13	4	9	8	3	17	21	7
Mixed patterns	1	1	1	..	5	6	1	6	7
TOTAL	39	36	25	64	45	31	103	81	56

Table 69 shows that the children whose behaviour was judged normal at the time of reception did rather well, and that the children with only slight manifestations of neurosis or delinquency were fairly satisfactory also. Between the small numbers of children in the main groups of definitely disturbed behaviour there are no clear differences—less than a third in each have done well, but very few children with mixed patterns (those who were aggressive, committed offences, and showed many neurotic symptoms) were in even moderately good condition at the end of two years.

As the numbers are small, caution is necessary in arriving at conclusions. The group of children, however, whose condition is classed as 'poor' is of some clinical and social interest, and a brief summary will therefore be given of the factors apparently responsible for the unsatisfactory outcome.

Unsocialized aggressive (9 children). Cerebral birth-injury, epileptic heredity, upbringing by a psychopathic mother, dullness without access to special teaching, and emotional turmoil demanding continuous psychiatric attention (which was available only after long delay) appeared to be chiefly responsible for poor outcome.

Socialized delinquent (15 children). Delays in effecting suitable placement, premature return home, parental indifference, and severe emotional abnormality in the child were mainly responsible.

Inhibited, neurotic (13 children). Apart from dullness and neurotic disorder that needed but had not received individual handling, the factors mainly responsible were physical defects, delays in placement, and lack of affection from parents or parent-substitutes.

Slightly disturbed, and normal (12 children). Unsatisfactory choice of homes and resentment about removal from parents were partially responsible. Some of the parents had been actively unhelpful. For example, a boy who had been deserted by his mother while his father was away in the Navy was placed in a children's home under the care of the children's officer. His alcoholic father, on return to civilian life, resented the court's refusal to give him unrestricted care of his children and encouraged his son openly to disobey the warden of the home and to run away.

Mixed patterns (7 children). Most of these children were not in touch with their parents and showed aversion, frustrated longing, or indifference to them. They had been in need of much psychiatric attention and very carefully selected alternative homes, but there had been delays in carrying out these recommendations. Some of the children were sent to the wrong type of home. The foster-parents of one child had so acted as to increase his distress at being parted from his family. Others had not been able to get the requisite psychiatric treatment or treatment had constantly been hampered by the opposition of the parents. These difficulties were in no sense due to lack of goodwill and effort on the part of the children's officer, child-guidance clinics, and others concerned; they were a result of unavoidable gaps in the existing services and of psychological obstacles presented by the child and his family. Two of the seven children had been much attached to their fathers who had died when the boys were between 2 and 3; the mother of one of them had remarried and thereafter behaved as though she rejected him.

The apparently adverse factors working against these children, who had differed in the extent and kind of maladjustment they had shown on reception, were very similar in the individual groups. They lay chiefly in the abnormal personalities of the children themselves, which had usually been evident very early in life, and partly in their circumstances. Lack of affection by parents or their substitutes, and remoteness of parents who lived so far away that there was no contact, were potent influences for ill. As far as foster-homes and various types of children's homes were concerned, the adults caring for the children were often unequal to the demands made on them, sometimes because they were only human instead of being all-wise, all-patient, and all-loving, and sometimes because they could not always achieve the necessary standard of sense and restraint. Some of the placements failed because frequent changes of staff deprived the child of security and of an enduring repository for his trust and affection. In addition to all this there was a lack of suitable facilities: facilities, that is, for special teaching when the child was backward; for psychiatric attention when his emotions were in conflict and his world awry; for putting him in the right sort of school, nursery, or foster-home suited to his peculiar needs. This catalogue of deficiencies sets out inferred, rather than proven, causes of deterioration: causes that were presumed, in the light of clinical experience and social probability, to have conspired against the children. The inferences may be mistaken; but this is perhaps less likely than that they overemphasize external influences at the expense of inborn disabilities or hidden psychological and social trammels. The respective effects are difficult indeed to disentangle. This study does not permit any confident statement on the matter.

(*h*) *Outcome related to pilfering*. Although it would be unprofitable to examine the persistency of particular symptoms (to specify, for example, how many children continued to bully other children, or how many wet the bed two years after they had left Mersham), there are some forms of antisocial behaviour which cause much trouble to the children themselves as well as to others. Stealing is one of them.

Stealing had been a prominent symptom before admission in 72 out of the 240 children followed up. Thirty-one had been referred to Mersham primarily because of it; 25 of these were

Subsequent Histories: Outcome

sent by the court with an explicit statement that stealing was the chief problem. In 41 others stealing, though troublesome, was not stated as the main reason for sending the child to Mersham.

When the later histories of these 72 children became available it was found that 6 had again been brought before juvenile courts for stealing, and one on a different charge. In all, 17 (24 per cent.) of the 72 had continued to steal; and 19 were socially unsatisfactory in other respects (usually lying or outbursts of violent temper). As opportunities for stealing are commonly greater for the child in his own home or a foster-home than in a hostel, residential centre, or approved school, the children are shown in Table 70 according to type of placement.

TABLE 70

CHILDREN SHOWING DISTURBED BEHAVIOUR DURING THE TWO YEARS AFTER RECEPTION RELATED TO TYPE OF PLACEMENT

Placement	DISTURBED BEHAVIOUR DURING TWO YEARS					Percentage stealing
	Stealing	Lying, violent temper, absconding	Neurotic symptoms	None	Total	
In own home or foster-home	9	5	5	3	22	41
In hostels, approved schools, &c.	8	14	12	16	50	16

Many of the children who were living in their own homes (there were few in foster-homes) were awaiting long-delayed places in hostels or residential schools; in other words, their homes had been considered an unsatisfactory second-best but no alternative had been found.

The frequency of neurotic symptoms is not fully shown in the table, since each child appears only once in it, and the third column contains only those who were showing neurotic symptoms without stealing or other disturbances of conduct. It seemed desirable to look for any confirmation of the impression that discipline and other measures may succeed in putting a stop to delinquent behaviour at the cost of reinforcing neurotic tendencies. Nearly half of the 72 children who had thieved or pilfered before admission had shown neurotic symptoms at the time of reception; two years later there was the same proportion of children with neurotic symptoms among the 55 who had stopped stealing. The view, therefore, that less pilfering may mean more neurosis was not confirmed.

6. OUTCOME IN 'PROBLEM FAMILIES'

Seventy-one children from 'problem families' (see Chapter 2) fell within the sample of 240 children followed up after two years. More than half were doing well. The condition of 24 per cent. had been assessed as 'good' at reception; two years later the percentage had more than doubled (Table 71).

TABLE 71

CONDITION AT RECEPTION AND TWO YEARS LATER OF SEVENTY-ONE CHILDREN OF 'PROBLEM FAMILIES'

Condition at time of reception	CONDITION TWO YEARS AFTER RECEPTION				
	Good	Fair	Poor	TOTAL	Per cent.
Good	13	3	1	17	24
Fair	15	9	4	28	40
Poor	11	11	4	26	36
TOTAL	39	23	9	71	..
Per cent.	55	32	13	..	100

The 9 children classified as in poor condition two years after reception included the following: 4 children who were maladjusted when admitted to Mersham and had remained so; 3 who had become worse while living at home with shiftless though affectionate parents to whose care they had been returned; a boy of 5 who had come to Mersham, with two elder and two younger sibs, from a discordant and degraded home after both his parents had been sent to prison; and lastly a boy aged 13, who did well for a year while living at an open-air school but who became aggressive and uncontrolled when allowed by the juvenile court to return home.

The children of 'problem families' did better than the other children in the follow-up sample. Apart from the important distinction already mentioned—other children were selected for

Subsequent Histories Outcome

admission because they had presented serious signs of neurosis and maladjustment, whereas 'problem family' children came for an extraneous reason, such as neglect, which had not necessarily harmed them psychologically—no further explanation for the difference can be found unless it is that fewer 'problem family' children had mothers lacking in affection.

Some inferences regarding the arrangements that are most helpful to these children—and to their luckless parents—will be put forward in the concluding chapter.

SUMMARY

1. Two hundred and forty children were followed up. They comprised all who had left the Mersham Centre at least two years before. In some the interval was three and a half years. Two methods were used—postal inquiry about all the 240 children, and an additional special inquiry, including a personal visit and psychiatric examination, of 50 boys and 50 girls consecutively admitted between April and December 1948.

2. The postal reports and the findings obtained by personal visit and examination of each of the 100 children tallied in 63 per cent.; in a further 23 per cent. discrepancies were either trifling or due to an interval having elapsed between the two inquiries. There remained 14 per cent. in whom the discrepancy was definite, though not wide; it was due, in all but one instance, to an unduly rosy picture in the postal report.

3. The proportion of children in good psychological and social condition had more than doubled during the two years or more since the children were at the Centre. Sixty-three per cent. of the individual children had improved, in varying degrees; 29 per cent. had had not changed; 8 per cent. were worse.

4. Neurotic symptoms had persisted to a greater extent than delinquent behaviour.

5. Children who had been placed in accordance with recommendations made at the Centre had fared somewhat better than those who were not placed as recommended. This was also true of recommendations about other matters such as schooling, contact with parents, occupation, and holiday arrangements.

6. Although there were differences in outcome between children placed in different ways (e.g. foster-home, approved school, or back in their own homes), no type of placement had a monopoly of success, and none had a generally adverse effect. In general, the closer

the child's contact with his parents or near relatives, the better his condition.

7. A mother who was normally affectionate—neither indifferent, nor averse, nor over-indulgent—was a prognostically favourable feature.

8. Separation from the mother before the age of 5 years was a prognostically adverse feature. Nearly a third of the children who were separated from their mothers were, however, in a satisfactory condition at the end of the follow-up period, and permanent separation before the age of 2 had not been the prelude to a particularly unsatisfactory condition of the child at the end of the period. Illustrative cases are described.

9. The outcome was better in children who at the time of reception showed affection for their families. Average or above-average intelligence was also prognostically favourable. Children exhibiting mixed patterns of behaviour (aggressive, delinquent, and neurotic) at the time of reception subsequently did badly.

10. Fifty-five (76 per cent.) of the 72 children originally referred for stealing had ceased to do so. A third of the 55 had been socially unsatisfactory in other ways (lying, outbursts of violent temper), and nearly a third more showed neurotic symptoms. Among the children who had stopped stealing, the proportion with neurotic symptoms was no higher, however, than the proportion among all pilferers at the time of reception.

11. The children who came from 'problem families' had improved, the proportion in good psychological condition having risen from 24 per cent. at reception to 55 per cent. at follow-up.

6

General Reflections

IN the foregoing chapters detailed findings have been presented and analysed in order to show who the Mersham children were, from what families they came, what their behaviour was like, and what came of the recommendations made about them. Little has been said of the atmosphere in the Reception Centre, the day-to-day problems of management, and the general impressions left by three years' work there as a psychiatrist. As there is obviously much of importance that cannot be reduced to tabulated numbers, and clinical impressions are sometimes useful where exact data are wanting, the following general reflections may be of interest to those who are responsible for similar centres.

The majority of the children were unsure of themselves, eager for adult approval, easily discouraged, and anxious to be with their parents; many who had been grossly neglected were, however, socially more competent and better able to stand on their own feet than the children of indulgent, over-solicitous mothers. The most striking and painful feature of most of them was their emotional upset—sorrow at being uprooted from their families, and fear of the uncertainties of the future; sometimes also resentment. These reactions raised in the minds of those who saw them the question whether removal from home could have been avoided, especially when it had been brought about just before they came to the Centre. How far this question could be answered will be seen later.

Because the children were disturbed by the change in their surroundings, it was very necessary that everything should be done, by kindly and perceptive management, to allay or minimize their concern at each stage of the passage from their old home towards the home they were going to live in after they left the Centre. Many of the practical measures this entailed seem obvious, but obvious measures are often overlooked. It is therefore expedient to review briefly the practice of the Mersham Centre, so far as it was designed to relieve the children's fears and grief and to help them to readjust to new conditions.

The child was told in language suited to his age and mental condition about his situation and prospects as far as these could be known. This was not a cold factual statement but a friendly and reassuring explanation; he was given ample opportunity to ask questions, which were answered truthfully. Sometimes he was in no state to take in an explanation when he arrived, but understanding gradually came later through discussion with a member of the staff. In these discussions much care was taken not to weaken or disrupt the child's love for his parents, even though the latter's failings or misdeeds had been the occasion of the child's removal from home. This cardinal rule was sometimes difficult to follow because of the attitude of the parents themselves towards the child's future. Often they, too, needed guidance, but some were too angry and embittered to accept it. Their state of mind influenced the child adversely. For example, after a period at Mersham on remand, a child would be brought before a juvenile court at which his parents, who had proved incapable of bringing him up properly, would display their resentment or distress at being parted from the child: when the child was then perhaps sent straightaway to a children's home or hostel, he harboured the same feelings of unhappiness and hostility as he had seen in his parents. In such circumstances it would have been better for the child, after the court's decision, to return to the Centre for a few days, in order to learn more about the reasons for the new arrangement and talk it over with an understanding but neutral adult (e.g. the warden), who would introduce him to his new home. It is self-evident that travelling to the new home with a familiar and trusted adult and receiving a pleasant welcome on arrival will ease the transition and help the child to transfer his affection and confidence to those who will henceforth care for him. Unfortunately, administrative arrangements did not always permit these simple and desirable things to be done. The administrative obstacles lay chiefly in shortage of staff, long journeys across the county, and short notice of removal. It seems likely that the continuous contact with an adult, which helps children over these awkward crucial stages of their readjustment, might best be attained by allocating each child

General Reflections

from the outset to an individual welfare officer who would be responsible for everything that had to be done for his ward by the children's department. That this would cost more than the present arrangement and demand more personnel is undeniable, but it would probably be worth it.

Telling the child about his next home is a delicate matter. The child's private hopes and fears, longings, and misconceptions are as a rule known to the psychiatrist; but, although they can be taken into account in putting the matter to the child, it is best for the child to be told by someone at the centre with whom he is in close daily contact—usually the warden. If, as suggested above, each child were allotted to a welfare officer, this person, if he were on a footing of close and easy co-operation with the staff of the reception centre, would be the proper adviser and guide at this juncture. The arrangement would also favour the termination of the child's stay at the right stage: too long a period at the reception centre is harmful because the child may then form strong attachments and be much upset when he leaves what he has come to regard as his new home; too short a stay defeats the main purpose of the centre, which is to assess the child's needs and recommend the best future arrangements. Without close collaboration between the child's welfare officer and the staff of the reception centre, the child either tends to stay too long in the centre, or, pending arrangements for final disposal, he may be shunted on to yet another interim home such as a hostel.

1. PARENTS

A child's happiness largely depends on the contact he has with his near relatives, especially his parents. In a few cases it would mar his well-being, but in the majority it is to his advantage to be in touch with them whatever the other arrangements made for his upbringing. When a child has been deserted or utterly rejected and realizes that he will always be unwanted, the question hardly arises, though even then it may in rare cases be good for the child to maintain some link with his natural parents, at least for a time.

For parents to keep in touch with a child who has ceased to be under their control something more than mere access to the child is needed. They must be not only permitted but encouraged to visit and write. Parents may make heavy demands on the patience and tolerant sympathy of the busy staff of children's homes, and if received coldly may not come again. In the child's interest, however, a warmer welcome should be extended to them than their uncouth, surly, or suspicious manners would ordinarily invite. So long as parents have a modicum of affection and sense of parental responsibility, the staff of children's homes can sometimes, by much perseverance and understanding, contribute greatly to changing or retraining them and so making it possible to establish some children again with their families.

This has a bearing on the question whether a child should go to a *foster-home*. If there is still a close link between him and his parents, it is unlikely that a foster-home will prove successful, because of the rivalry almost bound to ensue between the foster-parents and the natural parents (especially between the two mothers). A foster-parent will seldom tolerate or favour a continuing contact between a child and his real mother and father. On the other hand, when a child cannot for any reason remain bound by affection to his own parents, it is essential that he should be helped in every way to develop by degrees a substitutive relationship with someone else, who would most often be his foster-mother. There is today a strong move towards using foster-homes on a large scale for deprived children. This move is in the right direction but could be carried too far. However much this course is urged on grounds of economy or of psychological advantage, it would be unwise to extend it wholesale (if this were practicable) to older children who still look to their natural parents for company and affection, or to children who make exceptional demands because they are unresponsive and need more than average understanding and unremitting patience. Failings which would be overlooked or leniently regarded in a son or daughter may be severely judged in a foster-child. The results may be rejection, changes from one foster-home to another, and worsening behaviour of the child. For some such children a children's home or boarding-school is preferable. The Caldecott Community has provided a very successful residential centre of this sort; its children return to their parents during school holidays or develop alternative ties by spending the holidays with 'uncles and aunts' or in other private homes.

General Reflections

The child who has been deprived of parental love may be unable to respond with warmth to a would-be substitute: he may at first be shy and self-contained, for fear of further hurt; he may be hostile; and, at worst, he may be cold and repellent. Consequently he fits badly into an average foster-home, or indeed into any group that expects him to respond promptly to friendly advances, and he suffers if he is precipitately lodged with foster-parents who are avid for affection. As has been indicated in previous chapters, the truly 'affectionless' child is not as common among those long separated from their mothers as has sometimes been alleged. Reserved, unattractive, outwardly cold children may convey a spurious impression that they cannot give affection and do not want it from others; but this protective façade frequently hides a longing for affection and frequent stirrings of affection for others which the undemonstrative child dare not or cannot express, save in exceptional circumstances. Often, in talking to a child who had been removed from a foster-mother because she could not stand his apparently cold and unresponsive attitude to her efforts, I have been struck by the warmth of longing the child showed towards this home and foster-mother whom he had left years before. Such children need exceptionally understanding foster-mothers; so do recently bereaved children contending with their grief, and children who cling to the hope that they will be restored to parents who have, in fact, completely cast them off. The behaviour and outlook of such children may be transformed if they are entrusted to exceptionally gifted foster-mothers.

Many children presenting difficulties of this sort profit by further psychiatric advice at later stages of childhood and adolescence. Where this advice amounts to treatment, it is best provided by a child-guidance clinic or psychiatric hospital, but a psychiatrist at the reception centre, who is already well acquainted with the children and their problems, can deal with most of them. A personal interview with the child is not called for in every case: often discussion between the welfare officer concerned and the psychiatrist, as well as with other members of the reception centre staff, affords the needed guidance.

128   *General Reflections*

2. THE NEED FOR RECEPTION CENTRES

Although the Children Act required that reception centres should be established, and the Secretary of State, on the advice of his Advisory Council on Child Care, issued a memorandum[1] that emphasized the need for them and the lines on which they should work, there are critics who regard them as unnecessary or dangerous, except for a small minority of children coming under care. Such an opinion needs to be examined more closely.

The Home Office memorandum on reception centres put the argument for them in its opening paragraph:

> When a child is received into care by a local authority under Section I of the Children Act, 1948, or is committed to their care as a fit person, the best method of providing him with a substitute home cannot be decided without a close study of his needs as an individual. The children differ widely and will come from a great variety of homes, and it is essential that there should be opportunity for preliminary investigation, and for obtaining accurate and co-ordinated information about each of them. A right decision about placing, taken at the outset, will reduce the risk of subsequent changes and the disturbing effect on the child of breaking his relationships by transferring him to new surroundings. In order to obtain the fullest possible knowledge and understanding of a child's health, personality, conduct, intellectual capacity, emotional state and social history, provision must be made for his reception and temporary accommodation in a place where facilities are available for enquiry into these matters and for observation by a skilled staff.

The critics of reception centres say that the necessary knowledge of each child can best be obtained 'on an out-patient basis', i.e. at a child-guidance clinic or out-patient department of child psychiatry. They hold that admission to a reception centre is not called for and that it can be harmful. Their objections are twofold: information obtained by the reception centre procedure will be misleading, and the stay in the centre will have an adverse effect on the child and his parents.

These objections show a strangely distorted notion of the procedure at a well-organized reception centre. The first objection rests on a fallacious contrast of two methods of

[1] A Memorandum on the Provision and Conduct of Reception Centres circulated in July 1949. Appendix III. *Sixth Report on the Work of the Children's Department*. London, 1951. H.M.S.O.

General Reflections

obtaining information: (1) taking a detailed history and examining the child, along the lines familiar in child-guidance clinics, and (2) observing him after removal from his home to the new environment of the reception centre. To contrast the two methods is spurious since all the information that could be available to any child-guidance clinic is collected when the child is admitted to the reception centre, and is reinforced by data obtained through intimate contact with welfare officers and other social workers, as well as by the invaluable (and in many cases, one would say retrospectively, the indispensable) observation of the child's behaviour during his stay in the centre. But this last kind of information, the critics maintain, can be seriously misleading because children may behave in an uncharacteristic way in strange surroundings. A child's behaviour is characteristic of him in given conditions of time, place, and human environment; it can never be interpreted without regard to these, and no experienced observer would attempt to do so, any more than he would accept the odd contention that a child attending a session at a psychiatric out-patient department is more himself than when settled in a reception centre—nor would a competent observer accept the still odder assertion that a child's significant behaviour can be better observed in a session at an out-patient department, or on a brief outing with a social worker, than in the community life of a reception centre during a fortnight or more under steady but unobtrusive observation in a friendly atmosphere. The data given in earlier chapters, and the particular evidence afforded by children referred to Mersham after they had been investigated at a child-guidance clinic, indicate the value of the observations that can be made at a reception centre. The objection, in short, has no force unless the observers are naïve and unless those who collect social and clinical data about children in reception centres are negligent or untrained.

A minor but related objection is that administrators may come to regard admission to a reception centre as an easy solution of family difficulties and may resort too quickly to this disruption of a child's home life. Experience at the Mersham Centre suggests that this is a far-fetched idea: only a small proportion of the many children needing temporary care were referred to the Reception Centre, where the problem has been to find room for urgent admissions rather than to fend off children needlessly sent there. The administrators of the children's department of a county authority are commonly themselves experienced social workers or teachers, well aware of the diverse troubles they would lay up for themselves as well as for the children if they were over-hasty in removing children from their homes.

The second objection—that a stay in a reception centre may harm the child—is more deserving of serious attention. It is, on general grounds, preferable that a child should have as few moves as possible. The follow-up study, however, revealed that most of the children enjoyed their stay at Mersham, and that it tided many of them over the disturbing transition from their own home to another home, or a hostel or school. The children's officer for Kent knew of no instance where the stay at Mersham seemed to have done harm to a child (see Appendix 1). If the resident staff of the Centre had not consisted of carefully selected people, well suited to their exacting work, the conclusion might have been different: clumsy and insensitive handling would surely have added to the children's tribulations, and too close and long an association with the staff might have caused the children distress and disappointment when they passed on to the place where they were to live afterwards. The dangers can be overstated but cannot be overlooked. They are best avoided, not by whittling down the staffs of reception centres, or by abolishing the centres altogether, but rather by sound organization and careful selection of personnel.

There are, in plain fact, no alternatives to the reception centre. The alternatives that have been suggested do not yet exist on the scale demanded by the needs of deprived children. Child-guidance clinics, it is often urged, should provide investigations, diagnosis, and advice about placement for such children; but except in a small number of favoured localities child-guidance clinics are too few and too understaffed to cope even with their existing commitments: hence the long waiting-lists and delays, which would ill suit the urgent needs of the children whom we have been considering in this book.

On this question the opinion of the children's officer for Kent (see Appendix 1) is unequivocal. Asked if she would agree with the view that for the majority of deprived children investiga-

General Reflections

tion at a child-guidance clinic would be preferable to admission to a reception centre she wrote:

No. The continuous observation over a period of weeks enables a more complete picture of the child to be drawn than can be given by isolated interviews at child-guidance clinics. The observations on the behaviour of the children with others and with their siblings are very helpful in placing. The physical condition of a child coming into care is often poor though there may be no specific illness; improvement often begins to show during the stay at the reception centre and this is helpful in planning the child's future.

It is important for the specialists who are advising on placement to have an intimate knowledge of the practical problems with which a children's department is faced and this is gained more easily by those working in a reception centre than by those working in a clinic.

In a large county like Kent, geographical problems would be serious, all the clinics would have to be called on to do the work, and the claims on the time of clinic staff would be uneven and unpredictable. In a small compact area like a county borough it would probably be comparatively easy to arrange. It would also be workable if a reception home (as distinct from the specially staffed centre) were set up near to a clinic which was able to devote a good deal of time to this work.

Further it is suggested that instead of being admitted to a reception centre the children might be placed in temporary foster-homes specially selected for the purpose. Admirable as such a scheme might be for some young children (who were, in any case, seldom admitted to Mersham except when they were members of a family of neglected brothers and sisters whom the children's officer rightly wanted to keep together), it has demerits for some older children. Moreover, the proposal is unrealistic at a time when there is a serious shortage of suitable foster-parents even for normal children.

Another suggested alternative to the reception centre is the 'treatment centre for child psychiatric cases' which has been proposed as the best place for those who are very disturbed emotionally. It is a hypothetical proposal since hardly anywhere in this country are there facilities on the required scale, and it is unlikely that there will be, at any rate for a good while to come. The proposed alternative would, moreover, touch only a fraction of the children admitted to reception centres, unless

General Reflections

the criteria of severe emotional disturbance are made very liberal or esoteric.

The extreme view has recently been expressed (in a W.H.O. monograph[1]) that 'it is probably only for the older boy or girl who is a delinquent and a danger both to himself and to others that observation centres are really needed; these are usually called remand homes'. The experience and evidence, however, which have been accumulated at the Mersham Centre compel the firm conviction that reception centres, though not ideal, are indispensable at the present time for dealing with a large proportion of deprived children. This conviction carries with it the corollary that the essential problem must be tackled at its source—by finding ways to strengthen family life, by improving housing conditions, and by making it materially possible for mothers unsupported by their partners to give their full time to caring for their children if they are capable of it. It is not the object of the present inquiry to consider how these complex social issues could be examined and resolved: but prevention cannot but be constantly before the mind of any investigator who deals with the children sent to a reception centre.

Reception centres are necessary, but a bad reception centre is probably worse than none at all. To find entirely suitable staff for every centre is obviously very difficult. It is therefore prudent to assume that reception centres will differ, as schools and hospitals do, and that rules of universal application regarding their function and conduct cannot be drawn up. The ensuing suggestions are made with this in mind, and in the hope that, until standards are everywhere high, reception centres will be flexibily related to other services for children in a given region. The suggestions are therefore broad and tentative.

(a) Whenever the essential social, psychological, and medical examination of a child who may have to come into public care can be carried out, without detriment to the child, while he is still in his own home, this course is to be preferred to shifting him and making the inquiries later. It does not preclude the collection of further data, especially about his behaviour, in the reception centre if he should be admitted there.

[1] J. Bowlby, *Maternal Care and Mental Health*, W.H.O., Geneva, 1951, p. 137.

General Reflections

(*b*) The facilities for psychiatric assessment and advice at the centre must be adequate. Without them reception centres could easily regress into receiving homes of the old type.

(*c*) Close co-operation and easy exchange of information between the staff of the reception centre, the children's department, and the child psychiatric services of an area should be regarded as indispensable to the well-being of deprived children. It should be as common, for example, for the child welfare officer to be present at the centre when the placement of a child under his care is being discussed as it would be for a probation officer to attend the juvenile court in comparable circumstances. Such contacts should not be restricted to set occasions but should be informal, like the contacts between, say, a physician and a clinical pathologist; and they should extend likewise to voluntary agencies (such as the N.S.P.C.C.) and to the courts. The contacts could be about children still in their homes as well as about children already in the reception centre. If acted upon, this suggestion with the two preceding ones given above might sometimes make removal from home unnecessary, thus lessening the cost to the community and avoiding the stresses and strains set up when a child is removed from his family. The preventive aspect might thus come more to the fore, though it would be illusory to expect striking results in this direction soon, or even to expect that communication between the various people and institutions concerned with each deprived child could commonly be prompt, easy, full, and effective. The difficulties, however, in no sense diminish the importance of the objective. Among the benefits of co-operation focused on the reception centre are the educational opportunities it provides for all those concerned with children's care, and the full records which can be made available.

(*d*) Children under 5 should not normally be taken into a reception centre unless they are members of a family which must be kept together, or unless they present psychiatric troubles calling for close study. Occasionally however, it is advantageous to take into the reception centre a child under 5 if he has already been in public care for some time and has not settled in the home chosen for him.

No rigid age-limit should be set, but children under 2 should be admitted only in very exceptional circumstances.

(e) The number of deprived children over 5 years of age who are referred to reception centres must depend closely on the psychiatric facilities, hostels, and schools for maladjusted children in the region. It will probably always be desirable to admit the majority of those children who have been suddenly bereft of support (as by the death of their parents); likewise children of very cruel or hostile parents, or children who have been rejected from a foster-home at short notice. Emotionally disturbed and mildly delinquent children should also be admitted until in-patient psychiatric facilities improve. The number of children needing admission for any of the reasons just mentioned will fluctuate with the excellence of social and kindred services, and with the general state of society.

It might be expected that a survey and follow-up study such as is reported in this book would disclose whether the Reception Centre at Mersham had indeed justified its existence and helped the children. The findings reported in Chapter 5 permit some limited conclusions, but as they cover only two or three years of each child's life they tell us little. The story will not be complete until the children have grown up and become citizens and parents. For the present, reception centres must be judged in the light of general experience of their work, amplified perhaps by systematic findings such as it has been the intention of this study to offer.

Appendix 1

REPLIES BY CHILDREN'S OFFICER FOR KENT TO A QUESTIONNAIRE

(1) *Question.* If it had been possible, would you have thought it desirable to refer to the Reception Centre all children taken into care?
Answer. It would have been desirable to refer all long-stay cases. Some children of 'problem families' are received into care for short periods but come back again and again; it would have been desirable to refer 'short-stay' cases to the Centre once they had been recognized as 'recurring' cases.

(2) *Question.* If not, for which types or classes of children would you have thought it necessary?
Answer. Not for the straightforward short-stay case received into care because of the short illness or confinement of the mother.

(3) *Question.* Were there any cases where the stay in the Reception Centre seemed to have done harm? If so:
What types of children were harmed?
How was the harm recognized (i.e. what were the harmful effects)?
What did the harm?
Could it have been avoided?
Answer. No cases have been noticed.

(4) *Question.* Were the reports sent from the Centre during 1949-50 sometimes:
(*a*) Misleading?
(*b*) Superfluous?
(*c*) Too long or too short?
(*d*) Otherwise unhelpful (i.e. burdened with impracticable recommendations or unsound ones)? (Please amplify and give any details possible.)
Answer.
(*a*) No.
(*b*) No.
(*c*) Sometimes too short.
(*d*) Sometimes impracticable and in a very few instances considered by us to be unsound; these are, however, only opinions and I would rather not give examples.

(5) *Question.* Would the work of the Centre during 1947–50 have been more effective if the staff had been part of your department?

Answer. I think not. The children's department was not established until 1948 and it would have been impossible in the early days to arrange adequately for the staffing of such an experimental centre. It was also helpful to have the opportunity of consultation with specialists who were independent of the administrative machinery of a county council department.

(6) *Question.* Would you have liked more beds to be available at the Reception Centre? If so, how many (assuming an average stay of one month), and for what category of children?

Answer. Yes—about twenty-five more places for the children mentioned in (1). This would have enabled us to send all the long-stay cases without any selection.

(7) *Question.* It has been urged that for the majority of deprived children the necessary investigation, preparatory to placement, could be carried out quite well at a child-guidance clinic, and that this would be preferable to admission to a reception centre. Would you agree with this view?

Answer. No. The continuous observation over a period of weeks enables a more complete picture of the child to be drawn than can be given by isolated interviews at child-guidance clinics. The observations on the behaviour of the children with others and with their siblings are very helpful in placing. The physical condition of a child coming into care is often poor though there may be no specific illness; improvement often begins to show during the stay at the Reception Centre and this is helpful in planning the child's future.

It is important for the specialists who are advising on placement to have an intimate knowledge of the practical problems with which a children's department is faced and this is gained more easily by those working in a reception centre than by those working in a clinic.

In a large county like Kent geographical problems would be serious, all the clinics would have to be called on to do the work, and the claims on the time of clinic staff would be uneven and unpredictable. In a small compact area like a county borough it would probably be comparatively easy to arrange. It would also be workable if a reception home (as distinct from the specially staffed centre) were set up near to a clinic which was able to devote a good deal of time to this work.

Replies by Children's Officer for Kent 137

Some authorities are, no doubt, working along these lines now.

(8) *Question.* Is there any group of deprived children for whom you would consider the child-guidance clinic procedure better than the Reception Centre as a means of deciding placement?

Answer. Possibly for some children who are already well known to a child-guidance clinic.

(9) *Question.* Are short-term hostels necessary for children who cannot be placed immediately on leaving the Reception Centre or who need a further period of training and adjustment before being finally placed? If not, where should such children go?

Answer. We experimented for some months in running 'Southdowns' as an 'intermediate home' taking children from Mersham Reception Centre who were awaiting permanent placement. The staff complained that it appeared impossible to run such a home happily; there was a permanent feeling of unrest and anxiety among the children; each arrival and departure was disturbing; school arrangements were unsatisfactory. After this experience we decided that where it was necessary to make some temporary placing for a child from the Reception Centre it would be better to put him into the stable atmosphere of an ordinary children's home where the coming and going of an occasional child would not upset the whole community. We are fortunate in Kent in having a large number and variety of children's homes, so that this sort of temporary placing is probably easier for us than it would be for a smaller authority. From our experience it certainly seems that a disturbed child can become adjusted more easily in an ordinary children's home than in the special 'short-term' or 'intermediate' home.

Appendix 2

CASE-SUMMARIES: TWENTY-FOUR CHILDREN

THE following abstracts of case-records, together with others in the text, are given to show the background of some of the children referred to the Centre and the effect of their stay on them. The clinical details are necessarily brief.

'EDWARD'

EDWARD was admitted in February 1948 when 8 years 4 months old because he had been found in his foster-home to be disobedient, destructive, and restless in his sleep; recently he had been taking money from other children's pockets and staying out late.

His early life had been spent in most degraded surroundings. His mother had four children (all by different fathers) who lived with her in a filthy single room in a house with a bad reputation kept by her mother, Edward's grandmother. She was sexually promiscuous and left the children alone for hours. When Edward was 4 years 8 months old, his mother was sent to prison for neglecting her children. He was placed, with his younger sister, in the care of an elderly experienced foster-mother who had her daughter, a teacher, living with her. He had no further contact with his family.

At his foster-home he was destructive and occasionally difficult to manage but tolerable until a few months before admission to Mersham, when he began to steal small articles—balloons and pence—from fellow pupils at school. As his foster-mother feared that his sister would follow suit and had only reluctantly accepted him in the first place, she asked that he should be removed from her home.

After admission to the Centre he was restless, talkative, babyish, and quarrelsome. He met his elder half-brother (also then under care at the Centre), admired him intensely but fought him so much that they could not be kept together. He spoke with affection of his foster-mother, whom he had not wished to leave, but recalled no memories of his parents. His intelligence was average, his attainment in reading was good but in arithmetic poor.

In view of the insecure dependent attitude he showed it was thought best to place him in another home where there would be a foster-father as well as a kindly mother. This soon proved a failure as he was disobedient and defied his new foster-mother: after six weeks (during which he had been seen also at a child-guidance clinic) they asked for his removal.

He was readmitted to Mersham Reception Centre on 6 July 1948.

At first apathetic and forlorn, he became at times more sociable but also more aggressive. After three weeks he was transferred to a small adjustment hostel under an exceptionally able and understanding woman warden. Here too he was intractable. In December 1949 he was again referred to the child-guidance clinic where the opinion was expressed that he needed prolonged treatment in a school for maladjusted children. This recommendation was carried out, but within a month the headmaster and the physician of the school agreed that 'we can do nothing for him here'.

On his return to the adjustment hostel his behaviour was dangerous to himself and others. He climbed roofs; he disturbed the dormitory at night by shouting and banging; he was defiant, moody, easily upset, and unable to form any attachment to the people around him. This deterioration in his psychological and social state was manifest when he was once more admitted to the Reception Centre, and steps were taken to get him into the children's ward at the Maudsley Hospital. This was done on 1 May 1950, and he remained there for seven months, receiving active treatment which was later continued in the out-patient department of that hospital. He was next sent to a small cottage-home for boys, under a male superintendent. Much trouble was taken to ensure a smooth and undisturbing transition to these new surroundings.

Except for two violent outbursts during his first three months, he has shown satisfactory behaviour and has seemed happy during the ensuing two years. He is on good terms with the matron and the superintendent, friendly with the other children, and active both in team games and manipulative work, for which he shows much aptitude. He prides himself on his ability to bear pain stoically, a quality that he often exhibits in organized games. He has also been introduced through a hospital connexion to a woman who takes a regular interest in him and in whose home he spends holidays, which he enjoys.

This case of a boy who had grown progressively more disturbed after several placements illustrates the success of prolonged hospital treatment (in a children's psychiatric ward and later as an out-patient) combined with careful attention to ensuring the boy's smooth transition to his final home. This child, who was already feeling very insecure as a result of neglect and lack of affection, had been placed away from his mother at the age of just under 5 in a foster-home where he was not really wanted. Three years later he left this foster-home, but he continued to wish he could return there; his hostility to other women with whom he was placed increased and some antisocial traits developed.

Case-summaries: Twenty-four Children

'CHARLES'

CHARLES was admitted to the Centre at the age of 9. He had first come before the juvenile court when he was 7 and since then had been put on probation and brought before the court three times for stealing, staying away from school, and breaking windows.

He was the third of seven children. His father had recently been found guilty of receiving stolen property and his mother was an ill-tempered woman who had neglected her children for a time and frequently quarrelled with her husband. While he was away during the war she had acquired a bad reputation in the neighbourhood. Her two elder boys had been brought before the juvenile court and had been sent away from home.

In February 1947, shortly after his father had returned home from army service, Charles first came before the juvenile court. He was put on probation for six months and arrangements were made for him to attend a school nearer his home. Four months later he was accidentally burnt about the legs and thighs; he was in hospital for nearly three months and had skin-grafting operations. When he returned home he went to his new school, where he was friendly and well behaved though rather noisy in the playground. He did not learn well and soon joined one of his brothers in stealing. His parents were incapable of coping with the situation. They were in debt and were twice evicted for non-payment of rent. In December 1947 Charles was referred to a psychiatric clinic for delinquents where he was described as dull (I.Q. 88); the psychiatrist recommended that he should be committed to an approved school. The court, however, although aware that he roamed the streets with one of his brothers and had taken part with him in a number of thefts, put him on probation for two years.

No further delinquency was observed and the child behaved well at school until July 1948, when the headmaster, who had paid particular attention to him, was away. Charles then began to absent himself from school, was unresponsive to the efforts of the probation officer, and ignored the authority of his parents, who occasionally punished him. After his latest appearance in court, in 1948, he was referred to the Reception Centre for a full investigation of the causes of his delinquency and of his recent curious behaviour: he had been plucking his hair out so that his scalp became extremely sore.

At Mersham Charles's behaviour bore out what had been reported about him, but it also showed that he felt extremely inadequate. His rowdiness in a group, his capacity for creating a disturbance, and his lack of self-discipline and restraint were remarkable; he demanded from other children whatever he fancied, was resentful if

Case-summaries: Twenty-four Children   141

he could not have it, and constantly wanted to gain undivided attention for himself. Yet he was affectionate, and, alone with an adult, he was willing to admit his mistakes and became humorous and reasonable. In a psychiatric interview he was jumpy and tense, and showed the effect of his failures—he was discouraged, frightened and miserable. His intelligence was average but he showed little confidence and he was about $2\frac{1}{2}$ years behind his age-level in reading and arithmetic.

It was recommended that he should not return home but (as he needed prolonged individual attention within a small group) should go to a small junior approved school which would provide psychiatric advice and close supervision until adolescence; if this were not practicable it was recommended that he should go under a 'fit person' order to a small hostel for maladjusted children. It was urged that, whatever the plan adopted, personal relationships with the masters and teachers should be as close and secure as possible.

He was sent to a junior approved school conducted by a voluntary organization, where he lived in a 'flat' with a group of young boys under the care of two house-mothers for whom he showed little affection; but he sought out the headmaster and tried to gain his attention. During the ensuing years he did not steal or develop other delinquent traits. He did well at games but was restless and easily upset, and he absconded twice in company with boys older than himself. His reading and arithmetic improved but he was still behind his age-group. Although he visited his parents during holidays, they never wrote to him and he felt they did not want him. His affections centred on an aunt and uncle with whom he spent much of his time in the holidays and who would, he hoped, offer him a home.

A neglected boy, whose behaviour exhibited the pattern of 'socialized delinquency', had suffered from a sense of discouragement and inadequacy consequent on his being unwanted, if not actually rejected, by his parents. Placed away from home, he ceased to be delinquent but continued restless and unhappy.

'KENNETH'

KENNETH was 13 when he came to Mersham after his adoptive parents had found him to be beyond their control. They had complained about him for several years. Recently he had stolen some trifles from home and school and given them to other boys. The files of the education authority contained long reports about him from his 'mother', but in school he gave no trouble and mixed with other

Case-summaries: Twenty-four Children

boys moderately well; his work though fairly good was untidy and he found difficulty in concentrating. He had pilfered on two occasions, and at times sought the limelight.

He was an illegitimate child who had first been placed by his mother in various foster-homes, and was then adopted at the age of $4\frac{1}{2}$ years. His adoptive father was a quiet man who was in steady employment. His adoptive mother had been a nurse; she was a rigid, exacting, and dominating person. Finding him physically weak and backward when she adopted him, she concentrated all her skill on improving his health. He had not yet learned to chew properly when he came to her. He sucked his thumb, masturbated, and lay down all day as if he had been accustomed to be left in a cot for long hours at a time; he ate dirt and rubbish, slept badly, and had nightmares. As time went on, he began to steal a little from home and told lies.

His adoptive parents took him to a child-guidance clinic and he was then placed in a special foster-home where he lost most of his symptoms and behaved well. Unfortunately his adoptive parents, who disapproved of the free régime in the foster-home, withdrew him. They would not again co-operate with the clinic, but shortly afterwards they requested the education authority to place him away from home again. Finally they charged him with being beyond their control and he came on remand to Mersham.

He was found to be a boy of average intelligence, strikingly lacking in self-confidence though anxious for popularity and approval—so eager to gain the esteem of adults and other children that he became a nuisance. He occasionally hoarded trifles with which to impress others. He was easily hurt, and unusually clean and tidy. A 'fit person' order was made, and it was recommended that he should be placed under psychiatric supervision in a hostel for maladjusted children. This was not done because there were no vacancies, but he made good progress in an excellent remand home where he remained for nearly a year. No symptoms were complained of except his dreaminess, his pathetic desire for approval, and his studied politeness.

His adoptive parents showed no concern about him and wrote only occasionally. He was therefore placed with a kindly and experienced foster-mother, whose family consisted of husband, a grown-up son, and another son aged 7. He accepted this home, seemed happier and grew fond of his foster-mother, but his neurotic symptoms did not disappear: he slept badly, occasionally walked in his sleep or cried out in the night. At school he was regarded as a colourless boy who drifted along.

He was interviewed for follow-up purposes nine months after he had left school (2 years and 10 months after admission to the Recep-

Case-summaries: Twenty-four Children 143

tion Centre). His foster-mother stated that he was always honest and truthful but rather childish for his years and lacking in initiative. He experienced difficulty in keeping his jobs; he lost one because of dreaminess, and in his present job he was inclined to become angry and irritable if corrected. He had nightmares and slept badly, particularly after things had gone wrong at work. He was rather anxious about his health and self-conscious; he had grown lanky and thin and had much facial acne. It seemed that some of his troubles were temporarily increased by adolescence. His pleasure in coming home, helping his foster-mother and being appreciated by her, was evident.

A boy who had received inadequate care and no steady affection in early infancy was later submitted to a cold and restrictive discipline by his adoptive parents. He continued to show neurotic symptoms but developed much affection for the kindly foster-mother in whose care he was placed after he had been in the Reception Centre.

'ROBIN'

ROBIN, 9 years of age, the elder of two boys, was sent to the Mersham Reception Centre for observation at the request of a child-guidance clinic to which he had been referred four months earlier for having attacked and injured his brother with a chopper. The clinic requested residential observation. They suspected a psychosis because the boy had given irrelevant and nonsensical answers to their questions and shown restlessness and anxiety.

His parents got on well together; they and his maternal grandfather, an epileptic who lived upstairs, had made a great fuss of Robin until his brother was born five years later. His mother then made a favourite of the younger child although the grandparents continued to be fond of Robin. His parents stated that he had been a normal child except for occasional bed-wetting until he was 5, when he was hit and cut on the head by a stone. After this there had been a period of apathy attributed by the parents to the blow, although there was no other evidence of a severe injury. At this time his baby brother was learning to walk and to assert himself. Robin then had several outbursts of temper, but his parents were afraid to control or thwart him because the doctor had told them not to upset him. His jealousy of his younger brother became more overt. He began to injure his brother—attacking him with a knife, jamming his fingers in a drawer, and finally cutting his fingers with a chopper. By this time he had become very restless, bit his nails severely, and wet the bed. At school, however, the teachers made no complaint of his aggressiveness; he had learnt well once he had settled into the school routine. He warmed to encouragement but became inattentive when faced with difficulties. He was easily led into mischief and was not popular with other boys.

At the Reception Centre he was found to be of average intelligence but emotionally unstable; he did rather better on performance tests than on verbal ones. He was pale and slightly below average weight. In a psychiatric interview he behaved in a babyish way and commented inconsequently on objects around him, giving no information about himself in answer to questions. He approached strangers with demands to be lifted up and caressed. During the first two or three weeks at the Centre he seemed strained and preoccupied, emotionally much younger than his years and unable to care for himself. He cut up frogs and insects and attacked younger children. In school, however, he enjoyed his work, which he did reasonably well; he joined in games and in them was active and relaxed. After six weeks his behaviour outside school had also improved strikingly. He looked happy and interested and was willing to help other people: and he behaved normally for a child of his age. There was no evidence of psychosis. An electroencephalogram (taken in view of the family history of epilepsy and of his head-injury) showed no indication of epileptic tendency or cerebral damage.

It was felt that if he returned home immediately he would relapse into his old ways and it was suggested that he should be placed in a specially selected foster-home as the only young child—or failing this in a small adjustment hostel. But unfortunately no such place was then available and he had to return home. His mother decided not to let him go away again or attend the child-guidance clinic. After a few months, however, he started pilfering and was again brought to the clinic. She then agreed that he should go to a school for maladjusted children. While he was waiting for this to be arranged and attending the clinic, it became apparent that his mother was continually disparaging him, and he began to be rude and spiteful. Fifteen months after he first came to Mersham he was admitted to a school for maladjusted children where he settled down well. He stayed eighteen months and has since been getting on satisfactorily at home, attending an ordinary school.

This boy did not come from a broken home but was dangerously aggressive towards the younger brother for whom his mother had shown a preference. He was babyish, cruel, and emotionally unstable. Temporary placement away from home and psychiatric treatment helped him to overcome his hostility.

Case-summaries: Twenty-four Children

'IRIS'

IRIS, aged 6 years, was the illegitimate daughter of a mentally defective woman who had a mental illness when Iris was born and who had no contact with her after her ninth week. Her father was unknown. A maternal aunt was mentally defective and her maternal grandfather an unstable delinquent.

She remained in an institution until she was 4 months old and was then transferred to a public nursery. This nursery was a large one which offered good physical care and also endeavoured to provide each child with one nurse for feeding and handling. The matron had always taken a special interest in this child, bringing her to her home for holidays, the child calling her 'mother' and the matron's father 'father'. She was considered a lovable and very 'adoptable' child. When she was 3 years and 8 months old she was placed in a foster-home. Although the foster-parents thought her rather backward, all went well until a year later when the foster-parents, soon after they heard that her mother was in a mental hospital, began to complain that she had become silent and reserved and asked for her to be removed.

She went back to her former nursery, where her old spirits returned; her teacher considered her an intelligent pupil and she was very popular with the members of her class. She was referred to Mersham for advice about what to do next for her. She was there found to be affectionate and happy, self-confident, independent, and able to occupy herself well. Her intelligence was average.

She was placed immediately in the Caldecott Community, where she stayed for two and a half years, frequently being visited and spending her school holidays with a couple who were related to the nursery matron. She then went to this couple as a foster-child. Ten months later, when she was 9 years and 4 months old, the replies to a questionnaire sent to her welfare supervisor stated that she was on steadily affectionate terms with her foster-parents, had plenty of friends, occupied herself well, enjoyed reading, drawing, painting, and ballet dancing, and was in good physical health. The only criticisms made of her in her foster-home were that she was argumentative, not very interested in food, and that she had some slight fears of the dark and of witches.

In short, three years after reception this child had made satisfactory progress; the scars often attributed to early separation of a child from its mother and to institutional care were not demonstrable.

'VIOLET'

The development of this girl separated from her mother later in infancy (at 16 months) was less satisfactory than that of Iris. Her mother had herself been brought up in a children's home and had two other illegitimate children by different men; both these had been placed in public care. Violet was born while her mother was serving a prison sentence. After leaving prison, she took Violet with her to five different houses where she was employed as a resident domestic servant, but finally the child was admitted in a neglected state to a public nursery—the same nursery to which Iris was admitted.

Violet was frail and thin, unable to digest her food, and very backward. She remained in the nursery from 16 months to 32 months of age. A foster-home was then found for her with a sensible and affectionate young woman who had two boys of her own. Violet's physical state was at this time still poor; she weighed only 22 lb., did not chew solid food properly, wet the bed at night, and spoke unintelligibly. After four months her physical condition had greatly improved, but she wore out her foster-parents by constant demands for their attention and by running into danger through her insatiable curiosity. She frequently got hurt but she never seemed to learn from experience how to avoid accidents. Recently she had been seeking attention from strangers in the street.

On admission to Mersham at 3 years of age she still had the physical characteristics of a marasmic infant and her speech was poorly developed, but she was mentally alert and quite capable for her age—on Merrill-Palmer tests, four months above her age-level. Her abnormality showed itself in restlessness, desire for attention, and readiness to show affection to any adult, known or strange, who came near her. It was recommended that she should be placed as a single child with a foster-mother who could give her much individual attention, but a foster-home of sufficient merit could not be found and her previous foster-parents agreed to help her for a further period. They kept her for three months but were then so worn out that they requested her removal, and she was returned to her old nursery. Here her conduct steadily deteriorated. She became almost beside herself with excitement when strangers appeared, thrusting herself before them. She told lies, was spiteful to other children, and still failed to attach herself to any particular person.

She was readmitted to Mersham and it was found that her behaviour was too abnormal for her to be placed in a foster-home. Her overactivity resembled an adult hypomanic state. The voluntary children's society which was already caring for one of her half-

Case-summaries: Twenty-four Children 147

brothers was asked to accept her. She was admitted to their adjustment centre under psychiatric supervision, and there she made striking progress, losing her restlessness and much of her inordinate desire for attention. I saw her eight months later, when she was almost 6 years old. By this time she had much improved. She had good powers of concentration and got on well with other children, but she still indulged in fantasies of living again with her foster-parents. Those in charge were hopeful that she might eventually be suitable for placement in a foster-home.

In spite of this improvement, however, it was evident when I interviewed her that she was still unattached to anyone in particular. Although she was cheerful, played happily, and was superficially friendly, she was aware of her isolation. Asked to whom she would go if she were in trouble she said, 'I haven't got a mummy here. If I want someone I've Jesus and God.' 'But when you fall down and hurt yourself, who comforts you?' she was asked, to which she again replied, 'Jesus does.'

She spoke as if she had a mother and father who never came to see her: 'I've got a little brother at home with my mummy and my daddy and his name is David P——. My mummy doesn't know where this place is. It's in London and my mummy lives in my daddy's cottage.'

'Iris' and 'Violet'

These two children were both separated from their mothers when under 2 years of age. The first, Iris (like Nancy described in Chapter 5) had spent her early childhood in an institution and settled down satisfactorily in a foster-home later. Violet, who was maladjusted, though improving at the time of the follow-up inquiry, had been neglected until she was 16 months old and for many months was a sickly and wasted infant, unable to digest her food. She was too disturbed to remain in the foster-home where she lived for a few months at 3 years of age, but afterwards, though she was more stable, she regarded these foster-parents as her own parents and longed to be with them.

'ROBERT', 'MARY', AND 'ADA'

ROBERT, $9\frac{1}{2}$ years, MARY, $7\frac{1}{2}$ years, and ADA, 4 years and 2 months, came to the Centre in 1948. They had an elder brother who was mentally defective and two (twin) baby brothers who did not accompany them. Their parents had failed to improve the home conditions after a year's probation following a charge of neglect. The mother came of a family in which there was much mental defect in several generations; her brother and sister were certified as defectives. She was herself dull and indifferent, and unable to do her shopping or manage the household expenditure efficiently. The father was a cowman, a good worker, but dull. The mother's stepmother came to help the family after they were put on probation, but she soon left because she could not tolerate the condition of the home. At the time the children were removed all four rooms and the kitchen were in a filthy state and the furnishings were scanty. The mattresses were soaked with urine, stale baby's vomit lay on different parts of the floor, the living-room table was covered with grease and dirt, and the kitchen was disgustingly squalid. The babies were ingrained with dirt and wearing soiled rags. This state of affairs had developed only ten months after the family had been rehoused from much poorer premises. In spite of the neglect, there appeared to be normal affection between the parents and their children, and the mother was upset when they were separated.

At Mersham all three children were found to be normal in behaviour; the eldest, Robert, and the youngest, Ada, were of superior intelligence, both enterprising and rather sensitive children, fond of their home and parents. Robert was somewhat on the defensive and upset if a task was beyond him, compensating at times by boastfulness, but for the most part gay and well occupied. He liked to talk about his home and family. Mary was a simple happy child of dull intelligence (I.Q.81). Ada, the younger girl, was motherly and friendly but frail.

As it was unlikely that their mother would ever be able to care for them while they were young, an attempt was made to find stable foster-homes for the children near enough for them to meet each other and occasionally their parents. The foster-home chosen for Mary was a simple one suitable for her intellectual capacity. For the other two children foster-homes were found in the neighbourhood. These arrangements proved excellent for the two girls: when interviewed three years later, both were happy and identified themselves with their new parents and families. They often met and attended the same Sunday School; at long intervals they were taken to a family reunion with their own parents and siblings. Ada said that she never thought about her own parents and had no worries, but she appeared to be rather over-conscientious and a little self-absorbed. She blinked her eyes when embarrassed.

Robert had proved more of a problem. He had been quarrelsome with his foster-parents' son, and was later placed in another foster-home where his obstinancy and his open loyalty and preference for his own family caused annoyance. He said he had never felt happy away from home and asked to be allowed to return. Consent was given in July 1950 by the magistrates, but they did so reluctantly in

Case-summaries: Twenty-four Children 149

view of the bad home conditions and the inadequacy of his mother. He was seen at the follow-up interview after he had been at home for nine months. The welfare officer reported that although at times he was somewhat irritated and impatient with his mother, he liked to help her in many practical ways, looking after the new baby, to whom he was devoted, knitting, and growing vegetables for the family's use. He shared an interest in woodwork with his father, of whom he was very fond. He was doing excellently at school, where he always appeared clean and tidy, and the headmaster hoped he would gain entrance to a technical school. When interviewed he said that he was contented. It was evident that he was stoically accepting the limitations of his home. He was not prepared to hear it criticized and was resentful of offers of assistance. There were obsessional traits in his character and he had some anxiety dreams. He was evidently under a strain, struggling to rise above his surroundings. This strain might have been alleviated, had he been able to find a steady adult friend in the neighbourhood.

The chief problem in this family appeared to arise from the inefficiency of the mother. She was fond of her children but mentally inadequate. The eldest of the three children (all normal in their behaviour on first admission) resented being away from home and was later allowed to return without apparent detriment. The other two flourished in foster-homes.

'ROSE', 'BENNIE', 'TOM', 'JOAN', AND 'JOHN'

Mr. 'H.', aged 36, had been indifferent to the welfare of his wife and children throughout his married life. He spent little time at home and drank heavily, giving only a small proportion of his wages for housekeeping. His wife, a rather dull and nervous woman, who had apparently been pregnant when they married in 1938, was at first an adequate housewife. But as the family grew larger her housekeeping allowance hardly increased; she struggled on, reluctant to leave her husband, though her relatives advised her to do so. She had been over-dependent on her own mother and could not make decisions or face difficulties effectively. Her troubles mounted: there were many quarrels with her husband over money; their home was destroyed by bombs and in setting up a new one they got into debt.

In 1947, after the birth of her fifth child, the mother had a severe postpartum haemorrhage. She had no further medical attention after her return from hospital and remained anaemic, tired, and undernourished. Her own mother, who had helped her, died about

150 Case-summaries: Twenty-four Children

this time. She grew despondent, careless, and incapable of making any effort. She sat day by day idly in the doorway of her house, which was by then bare of furniture, dirty, and foul smelling. The children's clothing, too, was filthy. An unmarried woman with a young baby, who was dependent on the husband, had come to share one of the two rooms in which the family lived.

From early in 1947 the family had been watched by the N.S.P.C.C. and material help and advice had been given by the health department—all without effect. In 1948 the N.S.P.C.C. reported the family to the police with the result that the five children were brought to Mersham as a place of safety pending a charge of neglect against their parents.

At Mersham the four children, ROSE, $10\frac{1}{2}$, BENNIE, $9\frac{1}{2}$, TOM, 5, JOAN, $2\frac{3}{4}$, were shy and easily frightened though fond of each other and of their mother. The baby, JOHN, 1 year old, was apparently normal. Only one (Bennie) was below average weight. The eldest girl was timid, anxious, suspicious of adults, and rather dull; she occasionally wet her bed. Bennie, too, though of average intelligence, was at first anxious and over-active, wet his bed almost every night, and had frightening dreams, especially of being bombed.

It was recommended that the two eldest children should be placed in a cottage-home together, and that their mother, who seemed to have genuine affection for her children and was in such poor health, should be admitted with her three youngest children to a rest-home for negligent mothers where she could recover her spirits and receive instruction. She might then eventually be able to rebuild her home. This recommendation, however, was not followed. Husband and wife were convicted of wilful neglect, and all the children were placed in care under 'fit person' orders. The two eldest went to a cottage-home, the three youngest to nurseries. A further recommendation, that the children should as far as possible have contact with each other and with their parents, was put into effect.

Nearly three years later all five children were followed up by special inquiry and interview. The two eldest were happy and developing well. Their parents, now on better terms with each other, were writing to them, sending parcels, and visiting them regularly; they had had one holiday at home. The three younger children, however, were in a less satisfactory state. Joan had been shy and inhibited in her nursery for a long period; though improving, she was still generally retarded. Tom, too, was still abnormally shy and backward, and John, the baby, now nearly 4, was reserved, rather stubborn, and not closely attached to anyone. It seemed regrettable that these three young children had had to be separated from their mother.

Case-summaries: Twenty-four Children 151

Discord between parents and the ill health of the mother here led to squalor and neglect, for which the parents were prosecuted and sentenced. The younger children suffered in consequence of this break up of their sordid home, but the elder children are now doing well and are on satisfactory terms with their parents.

THE 'EDWARDS' FAMILY

The children of this family were NELLIE, $14\frac{1}{2}$, PAUL, 12, BERTHA, $10\frac{1}{2}$, DORIS, 6, and CHRISTINE, $3\frac{3}{4}$. An elder boy, already in employment, was not admitted to the Centre. Their parents had lived together for many years, but did not marry until 1943. The mother came from a respectable artisan family; the father was the black sheep of a well-to-do family. Although he had received a good education, he had failed in one business venture after another. Later he and his wife had taken domestic posts together, but they were dismissed for incessant quarrelling. Their last home had become filthy. The children ran wild, while the parents quarrelled violently. They were ultimately charged with neglecting the children and placed on probation. Eighteen months later the father reported to the police that his wife was sexually immoral and unfit to have the children in her care. On these grounds the court decided to remove them, and in 1948 they were remanded to the Mersham Centre as a place of safety.

When interviewed, the maternal relations and the children themselves told a somewhat different story. The father evidently had delusions of a sexual kind about his wife; he had previously ill treated her physically and kept her short of housekeeping money. She had become depressed and was hardly able to do her housework as she suffered from ulcerated legs and was constantly tired. She would sit about idly, smoking continuously, and she began to drink with her neighbours. The children had never had a settled home. They were often afraid that their mother would be hurt by their father (though they had some affection for him), and they did what they could to protect and help her.

On arrival at the Centre, they were dirty and unkempt, and the youngest child clung to the eldest. All five of them were frightened and over-serious for five or six days, but they were co-operative, obedient, and helpful. They often spoke of their mother and picked flowers to send her. The elder girls spoke of her as if she were a child for whom they must care, and their feelings for their father were a mixture of fear and admiration. The boy Paul was particularly attached to him and proud of his earlier position. Three of the children were of good average intelligence and two were of superior intelligence.

152   *Case-summaries: Twenty-four Children*

NELLIE, the eldest girl, although backward educationally, showed a social maturity beyond her years, enjoying domestic work and caring for others as if it were a vocation; she was tolerantly good humoured, and always careful and neat.

PAUL was a well-grown healthy boy, ambitious to become a draughtsman and intellectually equipped to do so, but a little retarded educationally.

BERTHA was less confident and emotionally equable than the other two, but she took part in the activities at the Centre with evident enjoyment, mixed well, and was motherly towards the younger two children.

It was more difficult to judge the personalities of the two youngest children, DORIS and CHRISTINE, because they developed measles soon after arrival and had to be temporarily separated from their brother and sisters. Christine behaved normally when she joined the other children. Doris was much incapacitated by severe bronchitis throughout her stay, but she appeared a lively and affectionate child by the time she left the Centre.

The main recommendations made for this family were that a 'fit person' order should be made; that the children be kept together in a foster-home or a small cottage-home where good educational facilities would be at hand; and that efforts should be made to rehabilitate their mother in the hope that she might eventually be able to set up a better home for them. The court approved this plan, but directed that the children should not see their parents for a period. The mother went to live with her own relatives, having obtained a legal separation from her husband, and she took a post as cook in an institution.

The usual difficulties were encountered in trying to keep such a large family together. At first all had to go to temporary homes. Then Nellie, the eldest girl, and Christine, the youngest, went together to a foster-home; a few months later Nellie became a resident student nurse at a nearby open-air school where her sister Doris had been placed. The second girl, Bertha, and Paul finally went to separate foster-homes not far away. Bertha was joined for a short time by Doris, of whom she became very jealous.

Unfortunately, the children felt resentful and unhappy at being separated from their mother. Nellie showed this most; she became listless and silent, and she defied the court's ruling by going to see her mother. After the court had made a concession and permitted her to do so, she recovered her spirits and became a capable and popular nurse. She was the leading spirit in keeping her brothers and sisters in touch with each other and, indirectly, with their mother. When I saw her three years later she seemed over-serious for her

Case-summaries: Twenty-four Children 153

years and all her thoughts at the interview were directed towards returning to live with her mother as soon as she was 18, and towards restoring Doris and Christine to her mother. She was already taking her to visit them and planning holidays for them all together. She still showed traces of resentment at having been prevented from keeping in touch with her mother after she left the Reception Centre.

Doris and Christine had not got on well in their foster-homes. Christine had at first been dull and withdrawn, then jealous of her foster-sister, anxious, terrified of change, and prim with adults, although she grew fond of her foster-parents and clamorous for their attention. She was readmitted to the Reception Centre in May 1950 and transferred to the adjacent Caldecott Community. When I saw her a year later she had become less anxious and was more secure in her relationships with adults and other children. She had been visiting her foster-parents for holidays; she looked on them as her parents and seemed to have forgotten her own mother. At school she was doing well.

Doris was readmitted to the Reception Centre six months after Christine because she had been unresponsive to her foster-mother, although she seemed normally affectionate at school, where she got on well. At the Centre she was superficially affectionate and sociable but anxious and over-talkative. It was decided to admit her also to the Caldecott Community. When she had been there for six months, she seemed happy to be with Christine but confused in her feelings for her late foster-mother and her own mother.

A later report of Doris and Christine is more satisfactory—they are happy and doing well at school. Nellie has helped to re-establish their contact with their mother, with whom they spend their holidays and who visits them at school. They come back to school each term without anxiety and accept the situation that their mother cannot have them at home because she has to go to work every day. They could not be fully restored to her owing to her instability of character and lack of a proper home, but the present arrangement gives great satisfaction to the children, to their mother, and to their 'mother-sister', Nellie. (Their father is now quite out of the picture.)

The position of Paul and Bertha is not quite the same. Paul is glad he was removed from his own home to come under the care of his foster-parents and has transferred his affections to them although he likes to hear from his family. He is a rather serious-minded, responsible, and sociable boy who shares his foster-father's interests and is about to become an apprentice to his foster-father's trade. Bertha is the least contented of the children. She has taken to her foster-parents and gives their surname as her own, but she is sensitive and resents any reminder of her own family. Occasionally she writes to her mother and brothers and sisters. She is of attractive appearance, well behaved and friendly at school but still rather backward educationally.

This family illustrates the difficulties of placing a number of brothers and sisters away from home without upsetting their relationship with their parents and each other. The two youngest children suffered most from the upheaval, but through the devotion of their eldest sister and placement in a residential school they seem now satisfactorily adjusted.

'CAROL', 'STEPHEN', 'ETHEL', 'BILL', AND 'SAM'

Five children, CAROL, aged 9 years and 10 months, STEPHEN, 7 years and 3 months, ETHEL, 6 years and 1 month, BILL, 5, and SAM, 3 years and 11 months, were admitted in 1947 from their home, a dirty ill-furnished hop-picker's hut. Two other younger children went to stay with relatives. Their father, once a stoker in the Navy, later a farm labourer but now unemployed, was a man who took life comfortably and wandered from job to job. But he was fond of his children and always gentle and kind to them. Their mother was a dull, shiftless woman, rather more assertive than her husband. She had lost her own mother in her teens, had been for four years in training-schools and then in domestic service until she had a baby, just before marriage.

After the marriage the couple lived in a number of farm huts, never settling for long; their family grew rapidly and since 1943 they had been receiving public assistance on and off. In 1947 they were destitute again and the children were not attending school. Their parents had been offered accommodation at the local institution but they had refused it because they feared being separated from their children.

The children were brought to the Mersham Centre at the instance of the N.S.P.C.C. After long efforts to obtain better conditions for the children the N.S.P.C.C. had decided to bring a charge of wilful neglect against the parents as the only course of action that seemed left to them. The children were well nourished and in good physical condition, apart from one with chronically infected tonsils and another with dental caries. Their personalities were pleasing; they were fond of each other and devoted to their father; they were independent and capable at practical tasks but educationally backward. The eldest, whose I.Q. was 79 on the revised Stanford-Binet scale, was of average intelligence on non-verbal tests; the others were

Case-summaries: Twenty-four Children 155

found to be of average ability on the Stanford-Binet scale. They settled quickly and behaved well at the Centre.

When the parents came before the magistrates three weeks after the children's admission, the charge of wilful neglect was dismissed. They were placed under voluntary supervision for two years and given temporary accommodation in a family flat in the old local institution, where meals were provided and the parents had to look after their children under the watchful eye of the matron. All five children rejoined their parents. The mother, who had been in poor health at the time they came to the Reception Centre, improved after her rest, and a month later was reported to be happy and managing her children and the housework well.

Shortly afterwards the family moved to separate premises where the home was kept reasonably well for a year. By this time another baby had been born and the other two young ones had come back to their mother. The father's employment was still irregular. By the end of the second year the mother had had a miscarriage and yet another baby, and the home now presented a picture of filth and neglect. The children and parents were dirty and ragged (although they were not ill or thin), and the older children persistently refused to attend school. They were ill-tempered and aggressive towards their mother; at school they were embarrassed by their illiteracy and poor clothing although they were usually well behaved. Sam, now 7 years old, occasionally had outbursts of temper and destructiveness at school after his mother had forced him to attend.

The five children were readmitted to Mersham in 1951 under a 'fit person' order, the parents having been charged with failing to send them to school. As was to be expected, they were all seriously backward educationally. In addition, the elder children were developing shiftless attitudes which had not been apparent before. CAROL, the eldest, by this time 13 years old, who had previously appeared capable and independent, now needed constant supervision to maintain her interest in a task; she was self-conscious about her failures, apprehensive about new situations, easily led and bullied, and her 'reading age' was only 6 years 5 months. STEPHEN, now aged $10\frac{1}{2}$ and suffering from tonsillar infection, was a cheerful, willing, and capable boy with some drive and aggression which was well controlled, but he was untidy. In school, where his 'reading age' was only 6 years, he had to be given constant attention to enable him to achieve anything. ETHEL, aged $9\frac{1}{2}$, spoke indistinctly and had little drive, but she worked well when helping an adult in the house. She did not seek the friendship of other children and in school she had no manifest interests. She was quite illiterate. Her score in a revised Stanford-Binet test was lower than previously (I.Q.85, as compared with I.Q.99 3¼ years before). BILL, aged 8¼, was pale and showed a pronounced lack of energy, with some signs of myocarditis. He, too, was quite illiterate and without interest or pleasure in school work, though of good average intelligence. He later became more active and sociable with other children in play. SAM, aged 7 years and 2 months, was more active, friendly, and cheerful than the others, and in school, though backward, worked neatly and with some confidence.

This follow-up inquiry was made shortly after their readmission to the Centre three and a quarter years after their first admission.

This was a large 'problem family' whose members were united and affectionate. An effort to re-establish the family failed, though they were given much help. The older children's social, mental, and physical condition deteriorated as the family increased in size. The children felt embarrassed by their disadvantages at school and refused to attend. They eventually had to be removed from their parents again.

INDEX

ABSCONDING, see WANDERING.
ADJUSTMENT HOSTELS, 8–10, 99–100, 108–9, 139, 144, 147.
ADOPTION, 28, 40, 70, 101, 106–8, 142–3.
ADVISORY COMMITTEE (Reception Centre), v, vi, xiii.
ADVISORY COMMITTEE ON CHILD CARE, HOME SECRETARY'S, 128.
AFFECTION, DEPRIVATION OF, see CHILDREN.
AFFECTIONLESS CHARACTER, see AFFECTIVE COLDNESS.
AFFECTIVE COLDNESS, 40–42, 46–47, 50, 75, 77, 83–84, 98, 105, 110, 112, 126–7, 139, 146, 153.
AGE, CHILDREN'S, 17, 36, 39, 44–45, 113–14.
AGGRESSIVENESS, see BEHAVIOUR.
ALCOHOLISM, 24, 31, 79, 82, 117, 149, 151.
ANDERSON, AUDREY, xiii.
ANXIETY, 36–38, 45, 47–48, 50, 67, 70, 80, 95, 109–10, 123, 137, 142–3, 149, 150–1, 153.
APATHY, 43.
APPROVED SCHOOLS, see SCHOOLS.
ARITHMETIC AND READING, 5, 35, 49, 115, 138, 141, 155.
(See also EDUCATIONAL ATTAINMENTS.)
ASTHMA, 25, 108.
ATTENTION, EXCESSIVE DEMAND FOR, 39–40, 42, 45, 47, 49–50, 96, 141–2, 144, 146, 153.
'AUNT' AND 'UNCLE' SCHEMES, 101, 126.

BACKGROUND, CHILDREN'S PERSONAL, 8, 28–31.
Influence on behaviour, 51–84.
BACKGROUND PATTERNS (see also FATHERS, MOTHERS, PARENTS), viii, 63–70.
'Constraint', 63–65, 67–69, 83 (see also DISCIPLINE).
Definition of, 52–53, 63–64.
'Neglect and bad company', viii, 63–69, 83 (see also DELINQUENCY, GANG DELINQUENCY, and NEGLECTED CHILDREN).
'Parental Rejection', viii, 63–69, 73, 83, 103, 111, 117, 125, 141.

BACKWARD CHILDREN, 8, 30, 81, 107, 115, 152–3, 155.
(See also CHILDREN AND EDUCATIONAL ATTAINMENTS.)
BARNARDO'S HOMES, DR., 20.
BEDWETTING, see ENURESIS.
BEHAVIOUR, 13, 87.
Aggressive, vii, 43–50, 53, 60–63, 65–71, 76–77, 80, 83, 116, 120, 122, 139, 144, 155.
Babyish, 39–40, 96, 107, 138, 143–4.
Delinquent, see DELINQUENCY.
Influence of family background on, 51–84.
Neurotic, viii, 5, 8, 9, 14, 17, 29, 32–34, 37, 40, 43–47, 49–50, 52, 60–63, 65–69, 76–77, 80, 83–84, 92, 95–96, 116–17, 119–22, 142–3.
Normal, 9, 33–34, 44–45, 48–50, 53, 55–56, 60, 71, 73–75, 80–81, 87, 108, 115–16, 120.
Patterns of, viii, 32–50, 60, 63–73, 76–77, 80, 83–84, 89, 96, 115–16, 119, 134.
Mixed, 44–46, 48–49, 50, 60, 68–70, 76, 117, 122.
'Over-inhibited neurotic', see BEHAVIOUR, Neurotic.
'Socialized delinquency', see DELINQUENCY.
'Unsocialized aggressive', see BEHAVIOUR, Aggressive.
Psychopathic, 9, 25, 32–34, 40–41, 49, 89, 105, 110.
BENDER, L., 105.
BINSWANGER, L., 40.
BIRTH INJURY, CEREBRAL, 116.
BIRTHS, 20, 28.
BLACKER, C. P., ix, xiii, 2.
BLINDNESS, 36, 48.
BOARDING SCHOOLS, 6–7, 9–10, 19, 64–65, 86–87, 92, 96–97, 99–100, 118–19, 126, 130, 142, 154.
BOWLBY, JOHN, viii, 41, 70, 75, 105, 132.
BRONCHIECTASIS, 36.
BRONCHITIS, 25, 152.
BULLYING, 39, 42, 46, 48, 95, 118, 155.
BURNS, 30, 140.

Index

BURT'S EDUCATIONAL ATTAINMENT TESTS, 5.
BUZZARD, SIR FARQUHAR, v.

CALDECOTT COMMUNITY, v, 1–2, 4, 8, 126, 145, 153.
CARCINOMA, 25–27.
CARE OF CHILDREN COMMITTEE, vi, viii, xi, 1–2, 12
CARE AND PROTECTION, CHILDREN IN NEED OF, 15, 45.
CASE HISTORIES, ix, 39–40, 45–46, 49, 74–75, 106–10, 138–56.
CENSUS 1951, 18–19, 22.
CEREBROSPINAL MENINGITIS, 30.
CHILD GUIDANCE CLINICS, 3, 8, 10–11, 13, 16–17, 28, 37, 43, 96, 107, 109, 115, 117, 127–9, 131, 136–7, 139, 142–4.
CHILD'S POSITION IN FAMILY, 29.
CHILDREN ACT 1948, xi, 2, 14–15, 97, 128.
CHILDREN (see also FATHERS, MOTHERS, NEGLECTED CHILDREN, PARENTS):
  Attitude of
    to adults, 38–40, 42, 45, 49–50, 88–89, 112–13, 146–7, 150.
    to other children, 39–40, 42–43, 46, 48–49, 67, 69, 88–89, 95, 108–9, 112, 144–7, 155–6 (see also BEHAVIOUR).
  Changes in condition of, 93–101, 116, 120–2.
  Cruelty of, 42–43, 46, 48, 144.
  Deprived of affection, viii, 24, 29, 31, 38, 41, 52, 54–56, 59–69, 73–74, 81, 83, 102–5, 110–11, 113, 117–18, 121–2, 124–7, 134, 139, 141.
  Dull or defective, 34, 68, 80, 88, 114–17, 140, 150, 153.
  Health of, 5–6, 8, 30–31, 35–36, 49, 68, 87, 101, 117, 142.
  In moral danger, 16.
  In public care, 8–9, 13, 15–18, 21–23, 25, 27, 30–31, 51–54, 58–60, 62–63, 82–83, 108, 132, 134, 146 (see also INSTITUTIONAL UPBRINGING).
  Intelligence of, 5, 34–35, 39, 49, 68, 80–81, 84, 88, 108–9, 114–15, 122, 138, 140–2, 144–6, 148, 150–1, 154–6.
  Mental health of, 29, 33–34, 56–57, 68, 77, 82, 89, 105, 110, 115, 117, 121 (see also BEHAVIOUR).
  Sexual misconduct of, 16, 47–48, 95.
  Under five, 2–3, 29, 35, 37, 41, 44, 54, 56, 60, 70–77, 82–84, 88, 105–7, 113–14, 120, 122, 131, 133–4, 139, 145–7.
  Placement of, 7, 133, 134.
CHILDREN AND YOUNG PERSONS ACT 1933, 1.
CHILDREN'S DEPARTMENT, see HOME OFFICE and KENT COUNTY COUNCIL.
CHILDREN'S HOMES, v, 7–10, 13–14, 20, 64, 68, 75, 86–87, 90, 92, 99–100, 111, 114, 117–18, 124, 126, 137, 139, 150.
  (See also HOSTELS and SHORT-STAY HOMES.)
CHILDREN'S OFFICER, ix, xi, xiii, 3, 5–7, 15, 27, 78, 86–87, 97, 117, 130–1.
  (See also WELFARE OFFICERS.)
CLAPHAM, BRENDA, xiii.
COLDS, 35, 108.
CONCENTRATION, CHILD'S LACK OF, 42, 45, 47, 142, 147.
CONTROL, CHILDREN BEYOND, 15–16, 18, 28, 80, 120, 141–2.
CONVALESCENT HOMES, 8.
COTTAGE HOMES, 7, 13, 111, 139, 150.
CRIME, see DELINQUENCY.
CRYING AND SCREAMING, 45, 107.
CURTIS COMMITTEE, vi, viii, xi, 1–2, 12.

DAVIES, ETHEL, xii, 2.
DAY-DREAMING, 96.
DEAFNESS, 30, 36.
DELINQUENCY:
  Juvenile, viii, 9, 15, 17–18, 32–34, 37, 42–50, 53, 60–70, 75–77, 80, 83–84, 89, 96, 98, 116–17, 119–22, 132, 134, 140–1.
  Parental, 18, 24, 31, 39, 79, 82, 120, 140, 144, 146.
DERMATITIS, 30.
DESTRUCTIVENESS, 16, 37, 42, 46, 49, 67, 95, 108, 138, 155.
DIRTY HOMES, 22, 28, 40, 53–55, 60, 64, 78, 80, 82, 138, 148, 150–1, 154–5.
DISCIPLINE, EXCESSIVE, viii, 46, 52, 63–65, 67–69, 83, 87, 119, 142–3.
DOMESTIC WORK, 2, 4.

Index

DREAMS, 37, 88, 142–3, 150.
DULLNESS, see CHILDREN, FATHERS, and MOTHERS.
EATING HABITS, 4, 95, 107.
EDUCATIONAL ATTAINMENTS, 5–6, 8, 30, 34, 81, 87, 89, 107, 115, 138, 141, 152–3, 155–6.
EDUCATIONAL NEEDS OF DEPRIVED CHILDREN, 11, 101, 114, 116, 152.
ELLIS, SIR ARTHUR, ix.
EMMINGHAUS, H., 40.
EMPLOYMENT (see also UNEMPLOYMENT):
Mothers in, xii, 20–21, 54, 60, 146.
Regularity of, 21, 31, 78, 155.
ENCEPHALITIS, 30.
ENCOPRESIS, 16, 37, 39–40, 47–49, 95.
ENURESIS, 16, 37, 39, 40, 46–50, 95, 108, 118, 143–4, 146, 150.
ENVIRONMENT, see BACKGROUND.
EPILEPSY, 25, 30, 33, 65, 68, 116, 143–4.
EVACUATED CHILDREN, xii, 29, 31.

FAMILY:
Allowances, 20.
Census, 19–20.
Incomes, 20–21, 31, 69, 78, 140, 149, 154.
Size, 19–21, 31, 69, 78–79.
FATHERS (see also PARENTS):
Absent during the war, xii.
Alcoholism of, 79, 82, 117, 149.
Criminals among, 39, 79, 82, 140.
Cruel or harsh, 54, 59–60, 78–79, 81–82, 151.
Dead or unknown, 23, 46, 52, 54, 60, 62, 74, 78, 81, 104–5, 109, 111, 117, 145.
Dull or defective, 79, 148.
Lack of affection of, 54, 59–60, 62, 64–65, 81, 83, 104–5.
Mental disabilities of, 27, 75, 151.
Neglectful, 54, 58–60, 82, 104–5.
Over-indulgent, 54, 58, 60, 81–82.
FERTILITY, 19–21, 31, 69, 78–79.
FILDES, LUCY, xii.
'FIT PERSON' ORDER, vi, ix, 10–11, 13, 15–16, 27, 52, 128, 141–2, 150, 152, 155.
FITS, see EPILEPSY.
FITZGERALD, MRS. H., xiii.
FOLLOW-UP, METHODS OF, vii, xii, 85–92, 121.
(See also RECEPTION CENTRE.)

FOSTER-HOMES, xii, 4, 8, 13–14, 17, 22, 52, 69, 74–75, 86–87, 92, 98–99, 100, 105, 108, 117–19, 121, 126–7, 138, 142–4, 146–9, 152–3.
Recommendation for placement in, 7–10, 114.
Repeated placement in, 30, 71, 75, 90, 109, 126, 134, 139, 142.
Shortage of, 7, 9, 13, 96–97, 131, 146.
Temporary, 131.
FOSTER-MOTHERS, v, 4, 53, 64, 70, 73, 88, 91, 108, 110, 114, 138, 143, 146–7, 153.
Cruelty of, 28.
Over-indulgence by, 39.
Rivalry between mothers and, 126.
FRETTER, F., xii.

GANG DELINQUENCY, viii, 43, 47–48, 63–69, 83.
GESELL'S NORMS OF DEVELOPMENT, 5.
GLASS, DAVID, 19.
GOLDFARB, W., 70, 105.
GOODENOUGH DRAWING TEST, 5.
GREBENIK, E., 19.

HARVIE, D. E., ix, xiii, 6.
HEART DISEASE, 25–27, 156.
Congenital, 30, 36, 49.
HEIGHT, 35–36.
HEREDITY, viii, 30, 51, 65, 116, 118.
HEWITT, L. E., viii, 42–43, 50, 52, 63, 66.
HOLIDAYS, 8, 100–2, 108, 121, 126, 139, 141, 145, 150, 153.
HOME OFFICE, CHILDREN'S DEPARTMENT, 128.
HOME, PARENTAL:
Child's removal from, viii, ix, 13, 27, 30–31, 33, 37, 52, 78, 81, 91, 117, 123–4, 129–30, 133, 156.
Child's repeated removal from, 29–31.
Child's return to, 8–11, 13–14, 99–102, 114, 117, 120–1, 153.
HOSPITALS, 5, 8, 25, 27, 30, 35, 88, 127, 139–40.
Out-patient departments, 128–9, 139.
HOSTELS, 7, 13, 87, 107–8, 111, 119, 124, 130, 141–2.
(See also ADJUSTMENT HOSTELS and CHILDREN'S HOMES.)

Housing, xii, 3, 22, 31, 97, 132, 148, 155.
Hypomania, 146.

Illegitimacy, 11, 19, 22–23, 25, 28–29, 31, 40, 49, 51, 54, 60, 63, 74–75, 83, 106, 108, 145–6, 154.
Illiteracy, 34, 155–6.
(See also Educational Attainments.)
Impetigo, 35.
Infections, 35.
Injuries, 25, 30.
Institutional Upbringing, 15, 17, 22, 39, 41, 51–52, 70–71, 73–75, 88, 100, 105, 108, 111, 145, 147.
Intelligence, see Children, Fathers, Mothers, and Parents.
'Intermediate Home', 137.

Jamieson, K. E., xiii.
Jenkins, R. L., viii, 42–43, 50, 52, 63, 66.
Jennings, M., 5.
Juvenile Courts, 3, 5, 7, 14–15, 17, 37, 40, 81, 117, 119–20, 124, 133, 140, 148, 152, 155.
Juvenile Delinquency, see Delinquency.

Kent County Council, vii, 2.
Children's department, vi–viii, xiii, 3, 11, 15, 88, 125, 136 (see also Children's Officer).
Education Department, xiii, 3, 14–16, 141–2.
Health department, 150.
Public assistance committee, 15.
Kline, I., xiii.
Kline, M., xiii.
Koh's Blocks, 5, 34.

Lewis, Aubrey, xiii.
Leys, Duncan, 5, 35.
Lowrey, L., 105.
Lying, 38, 47, 95, 119, 122, 142, 146.

Magistrates, see Juvenile Courts.
Maladjustment, 8–9, 14, 16–17, 38, 42, 51–52, 89, 96, 107, 118, 120–1, 147.
(See also Behaviour and Schools.)
Mannerisms, 38, 46, 95.
Masturbation, 38, 142.

Maudsley Hospital, 139.
Measles, 36, 152.
Medical Care, 5–6, 10, 101.
(See also Hospitals.)
Meningitis, 30.
Mental Disabilities, see Children, Fathers, Mothers, Parents.
Mental Hospitals, 25, 27.
Merrill-Palmer Test, 5, 34, 146.
Michigan Child Guidance Institute, 42.
Ministry of Health, 2.
'Moral Insanity', 40.
Mortality, 19–20.
Mother, Separation from, 29, 31, 69–77, 81–84, 105–12, 122, 152.
Children under five, 29, 41, 54, 56, 60, 70–77, 82–84, 105–7, 122, 139, 145–7.
Permanently, 29, 31, 70–74, 76, 82–84, 105–7, 110.
Temporarily, 70–73, 76, 105–7.
Mother-substitutes, 51, 59, 64, 70, 73–75, 89, 105, 111–13, 117–18, 126–7.
(See also Foster-mothers.)
Mothers (see also Parents):
Alcoholism of, 82, 151.
Confinement of, 12, 27, 149.
Criminals among, 82, 146.
Cruel or harsh, 28, 60, 81.
Dead or unknown, 23, 27, 54–55, 59–60, 62, 74, 78, 81–82, 103–4.
Deserted, divorced, or widowed, 23, 27, 132.
Desertion of children by, 23, 73–75, 81, 103–4, 117.
Dull or defective, 39, 54, 56–57, 60, 79, 82–83, 145, 147–9, 154.
Health of, 27–28, 54, 60, 72, 79, 149, 151, 155.
In employment, xii, 20–21, 54, 60, 146.
Intelligence of, 28, 39, 54, 56–57, 60, 79, 82–83, 145, 147–9, 154.
Lack of affection of, 29, 41, 54–56, 60, 62, 64–65, 81, 83, 103, 110–11, 113, 121–2.
Mental disabilities of, 39, 54, 57, 60–61, 74, 79, 82–83, 88, 107, 109, 116, 145, 147–9, 154.
Neglectful, 11, 28, 54–57, 59–60, 74, 82, 103–4, 138, 140–1, 146–50.

Index

Over-indulgent, 54, 57–60, 81–82, 103, 122–3.
Rest homes for, 150.
Sexual laxity of, 49, 54, 60, 79, 82, 138, 151.
MYOCARDITIS, 156.

NAIL-BITING, 37–38, 47, 143–4.
NASAL DISCHARGE, CHRONIC, 36.
NATIONAL SOCIETY FOR THE PREVENTION OF CRUELTY TO CHILDREN, 3–4, 17–18, 78, 133, 150, 154.
NEGLECTED CHILDREN, viii, 4, 8, 11, 16–17, 20, 22, 27–28, 40, 45, 52–60, 63–69, 74, 77–78, 81–83, 101, 103–5, 121, 123, 131, 138–41, 146–51, 154–5.
(*See also* 'PROBLEM FAMILIES' and DIRTY HOMES.)
NEUROTIC CHILDREN, *see* BEHAVIOUR.
NIGHTMARES, 37, 88, 142–3, 150.
NUFFIELD FOUNDATION, v, 2.
NURSERIES, 3, 27, 29–30, 39, 99–100, 106–8, 111, 118, 145–6, 150.

OBSESSIONAL TRAITS, 38, 47, 95.
OPEN AIR SCHOOLS, *see* SCHOOLS.
OSTRACISM, 40, 64, 80.
OTITIS MEDIA, 30, 36.
OVERCROWDING, 22, 31.

PARENTS (*see also* FATHERS and MOTHERS), 3, 13, 22–28, 88, 125–7.
Absence of, caused by death or desertion, 7, 16, 23, 25, 31, 51, 53, 64, 74, 91, 114, 125, 127, 134.
Affectionate but incompetent, 8, 24–25, 81–82, 101, 120.
Alcoholism of, 24, 31.
And relatives, children in contact with, 6, 8, 10, 64, 87, 89, 91, 100–2, 113, 117–18, 121–2, 125–6, 138, 150–1, 153–4.
Children's attitude to, 4–5, 81, 111–13, 122–4, 148, 150, 154.
Criminals among, 24, 31, 120.
Cruelty of, 16–17, 23–24, 28, 31, 103, 134.
Health of, 3, 18, 22, 24–27, 31, 64, 72, 79.
Intelligence of, 6, 18, 25–26, 31, 51, 84.
Lack of affection of, viii, 24, 31, 52, 63–69, 73–74, 81, 83, 102–3, 111, 117–18, 124–7, 134, 139, 141.

Mental disabilities of, 5–6, 25–27, 31, 51, 57, 79, 101.
Neglectful, 4, 24, 27, 81, 101, 151.
  convicted, 101, 150–1.
  on probation, 11, 140, 147, 151.
  Over-indulgent, 24, 64.
Relationship between, 22–24, 29, 31, 54, 60, 78, 82, 84, 101, 120, 140, 148–51.
Separation from, 5, 8, 12, 29, 51, 64, 105 (*see also* MOTHER, SEPARATION FROM).
Sexual misconduct by, 23–25, 31, 75.
Social defects of, 6, 8, 18, 22, 24–25, 31, 51, 81–82, 84, 101, 117, 120.
PENSIONS, 20.
PERFORMANCE TESTS, 35, 49.
(*See also* READING AND ARITHMETIC.)
PHYSICAL TRAINING, 2, 4.
PILFERING, 16–17, 37–38, 40, 42–43, 46–50, 67, 77, 91, 95, 109, 118–20, 122, 138, 140–2, 144.
'PLACE OF SAFETY' ORDER, 13, 150.
PLACEMENTS (*see also* CHILDREN'S HOMES, FOSTER HOMES, SCHOOLS), 6–11, 14, 53, 86, 96–7, 113–14, 117, 121, 128, 133.
Changes in, 30, 71, 73, 75, 87, 90–91, 98–99, 105, 108–9, 118, 126, 128, 134, 139, 142.
Delays in, 96–98, 101, 117, 119.
Of family groups, 100, 114.
Outcome related to, 97–101.
POTT'S DISEASE, 30.
PROBATION OFFICERS, 3–5, 28, 89, 133, 140.
'PROBLEM FAMILIES', 18, 20–22, 24, 33, 40, 51, 53, 63, 72, 77–84, 120–2, 135, 154–6.
PROGRESSIVE MATRICES TEST, 5, 34.
PSYCHIATRIC HOSPITALS, 8, 88, 127.
Out-patient departments of, 128–9, 139.
PSYCHIATRIC SOCIAL WORKERS, xii, 3–4, 6, 18, 86–87.
PSYCHIATRIST, vii, 5–7, 11, 13, 32, 86, 88, 115, 127.
PSYCHIATRY, 2, 40, 65, 96, 116, 133–4, 140–2, 144, 147.
PSYCHOLOGISTS, EDUCATIONAL, 6, 11.
PSYCHOPATHIC PERSONALITY, *see* BEHAVIOUR.
PUBLIC ASSISTANCE, 15, 154.

162 Index

PUERPERAL MANIA, 109.
PULMONARY ABSCESS, 30.

READING AND ARITHMETIC, 5, 35, 49, 115, 138, 141, 155.
(*See also* EDUCATIONAL ATTAINMENTS.)
RECEPTION CENTRE:
Admissions to, 3–5, 11, 15–31, 53, 71.
causes of, 16–17, 30.
children in family groups, 7, 9, 18, 52, 79–81, 100, 114, 120, 131, 133, 147–56.
Case conferences at, 5, 9.
Discharges from, 11, 13, 85.
Duration of stay at, 11–12, 14,
Establishment of, 2, 123–5.
Functions of, vi, ix, xi, 1–14, 132–7.
Matron of, 2, 4.
Need for, v–vi, ix, 128–37.
Opposition to, 128–32.
Outcome of work done by, 85–122.
Recommendations made by, vi, 6–8, 14, 87, 96–97.
action taken on, 93–102, 121, 150.
Warden of, xii, 2–4, 6, 124–5.
REMAND HOMES, 15, 132, 142.
RENDEL, LEILA, v, xii, 2.
RETARDED CLASSES IN ORDINARY SCHOOLS, 11, 115.
RICHARDSON, M., xiii.
RORSCHACH TESTS, 74.
ROYAL COMMISSION ON POPULATION, 19.

SCARLET FEVER, 36.
SCHIZOPHRENIA, 47.
SCHLEICHER, H. J., xii.
SCHOOL INQUIRY OFFICERS, 4, 28.
SCHOOL MEDICAL OFFICERS, 16.
SCHOOLS (*see also* BOARDING SCHOOLS *and* TEACHERS), 4, 11, 30, 115, 121, 142, 144, 149, 153.
Approved, v, 9–10, 87, 92, 98–99, 106, 119, 121, 140–1.
Changes of, 30–31, 34, 91.
For educationally subnormal children, 8–10, 13, 99–100.
For maladjusted children, 8–10, 13, 40, 88, 97, 99–100, 134, 139, 141–2, 144 (*see also* MALADJUSTMENT).
Open air, 8, 120.
SELF-INJURY, 48.
SEPARATION FROM MOTHER, *see* MOTHER.

SEXUAL MISCONDUCT:
Children, 16, 47–48, 95.
Parents, 23–25, 31, 49, 54, 60, 75, 79, 82, 138, 151.
SHORT-STAY CASES, vi, 12, 27, 72, 135.
SHORT-STAY HOMES, 1, 27, 137.
SHORTAGE OF:
Accommodation for children, 6–7, 11, 13–14, 96–97, 109, 117–18, 124, 130, 136.
Foster-homes, 7, 9, 13, 96–97, 131, 146.
Places in schools, 6, 96–97, 142.
SHYNESS, 40, 43, 46–48, 67, 95, 127, 150.
'SIBLING RIVALRY', 68–70, 109, 143–4, 153.
SLEEP, 4, 37, 47–48, 88, 95, 138, 142–3.
SLUMS, 64, 67, 77.
SOCIAL CLASS, 18–19, 31, 78.
SOCIAL WORKERS, 4, 13, 129–30.
(*See also* PSYCHIATRIC SOCIAL WORKERS *and* WELFARE OFFICERS.)
SOILING, *see* ENCOPRESIS.
SPITZ, R., 105.
STAMMERING, 96.
STANFORD-BINET TEST, 5, 34–35, 49, 80, 154–5.
STEALING, *see* PILFERING.
STEP-PARENTS, 64, 69.
STILLBIRTHS, 19.

TANTRUMS, 39, 41, 43, 46, 67, 95, 108, 110, 119, 122, 139, 143, 155.
TEACHERS, 2–4, 6, 18, 34, 87, 108, 115, 130, 141, 144.
THATCHER, B., xiii.
THUMB-SUCKING, 47, 142.
TONSILS, INFECTED, 154–5.
TRUANCY, 16, 40, 43, 95, 140, 155–6.
TUBERCULOSIS, 24–27, 36.

UNEMPLOYMENT, 21–22, 78–79, 154.

VOCATIONAL GUIDANCE, 6, 10, 101.
VOLUNTARY BODIES, 3, 7, 133, 141, 146, 155.
(*See also* CALDECOTT COMMUNITY *and* NATIONAL SOCIETY FOR THE PREVENTION OF CRUELTY TO CHILDREN.)

WALKER, K., xii.

WANDERING, 12–13, 16, 38–40, 43, 46, 48, 50, 67, 95, 107, 119, 141.
WAR, xii, 29–31, 51–52.
(*See also* EVACUATED CHILDREN.)
WATSON, AUDREY, xii.
WEIGHT, 35–36, 49, 108, 144, 146.
WELFARE AUTHORITIES, vi, 3, 128, 130–1, 133, 136.
(*See also* KENT COUNTY COUNCIL.)

WELFARE OFFICERS, viii, 3, 5–6, 13–14, 18, 85–88, 97, 125, 127, 129, 138, 149.
(*See also* CHILDREN'S OFFICER.)
WHOOPING COUGH, 36.
WOLLEN, C. A., xii.
WOODS, D., xii–xiii.

ZIEHEN, TH., 40.